# *The Healing Dialogue*

## Empowering Conversations for Lasting Change and Personal Development

## Rita Nunez

The presentation of the information is without contract or any type of guarantee assurance. The trademarks that are used are without any consent, and the publication of the trademark is without permission or backing by the trademark owner. All trademarks and brands within this book are for clarifying purposes only and are the owned by the owners themselves, not affiliated with this document.

# Table of Contents

# Chapter 1

# Introduction to Healing Dialogue

## The Essence of Empowering Conversations

Empowering conversations are the cornerstone of transformative relationships, whether in personal or professional settings. These dialogues are not merely exchanges of words but are profound interactions that can inspire change, foster growth, and build deeper connections. At their core, empowering conversations are about creating a space where individuals feel heard, valued, and motivated to explore their potential. This chapter delves into the essence of such conversations, exploring the elements that make them effective and transformative.

The foundation of an empowering conversation lies in the intention behind it. Unlike ordinary dialogues, these conversations are driven by a purpose that transcends mere information exchange. The intention is to uplift, support, and guide the other person towards a path of self-discovery and growth. This requires a mindset shift from simply communicating to actively engaging with the other person's thoughts, feelings, and aspirations. The focus is on understanding and facilitating the other person's journey, rather than imposing one's own agenda.

Active listening is a critical component of empowering conversations. It involves more than just hearing the words spoken; it requires a deep engagement with the speaker's message, both verbal and nonverbal. Active listening means being fully present in the moment, setting aside distractions, and giving undivided attention to the speaker. It involves acknowledging the speaker's emotions and responding with empathy and understanding. By doing so, the listener creates a safe and supportive environment where the speaker feels comfortable expressing themselves openly and honestly.

Empathy plays a pivotal role in empowering conversations. It is the ability to understand and share the feelings of another person, to see the world through their eyes. Empathy allows the listener to connect with the speaker on a deeper level, fostering trust and rapport. When individuals feel understood and validated, they are more likely to open up and explore their thoughts and emotions. This openness is essential for personal growth and development, as it encourages individuals to confront their challenges and seek solutions.

The language used in empowering conversations is also crucial. Words have the power to uplift or diminish, to inspire or discourage. In these conversations, the language should be positive, encouraging, and supportive. It should focus on possibilities and potential, rather than limitations and obstacles. The use of open-ended questions can be particularly effective, as they invite the speaker to reflect and explore their thoughts and feelings more deeply. These questions encourage self-discovery and insight, empowering the speaker to find their own answers and solutions.

Creating a safe and non-judgmental space is essential for empowering conversations. Individuals need to feel that they can express themselves without fear of criticism or judgment. This requires the listener to adopt a stance of openness and acceptance, embracing the speaker's perspective without imposing their own biases or assumptions. By fostering an environment of trust and respect, the listener encourages the speaker to be vulnerable and authentic, paving the way for meaningful and transformative dialogue.

Empowering conversations are not one-sided; they are collaborative and dynamic interactions. Both parties contribute to the dialogue, sharing their thoughts, experiences, and insights. This collaboration fosters a sense of partnership and mutual respect, where both individuals feel valued and heard. The listener's role is to guide and support the speaker, helping them to explore their thoughts and emotions, while also offering their own perspectives and insights when appropriate.

The impact of empowering conversations extends beyond the immediate interaction. These dialogues have the potential to inspire lasting change and personal development. By encouraging individuals to reflect on their experiences and explore new possibilities, empowering conversations can lead to increased self-awareness, confidence, and resilience. They can help individuals to identify their strengths and areas for growth, setting the stage for positive change and transformation.

# The Role of Dialogue in Personal Development

Dialogue serves as a powerful catalyst for personal development, acting as a bridge between self-awareness and growth. It is through meaningful conversations that individuals can explore their thoughts, emotions, and experiences, gaining insights that propel them forward on their journey of self-improvement. The role of dialogue in personal development is multifaceted, encompassing self-reflection, learning, and transformation.

At the heart of personal development lies the ability to understand oneself better. Dialogue provides a mirror through which individuals can examine their beliefs, values, and behaviors. Engaging in conversations with others allows for the exchange of perspectives, challenging preconceived notions and encouraging introspection. This process of self-reflection is crucial for personal growth, as it enables individuals to identify areas for improvement and recognize their strengths.

One of the most significant aspects of dialogue in personal development is its capacity to foster self-awareness. Through conversations, individuals can gain a deeper understanding of their emotions, motivations, and desires. This heightened self-awareness is essential for making informed decisions and setting meaningful goals. By articulating thoughts and feelings in dialogue, individuals can clarify their intentions and align their actions with their values.

Dialogue also plays a vital role in learning and acquiring new knowledge. Conversations with others provide opportunities to gain insights and information that may not be accessible through solitary reflection. Engaging with diverse perspectives broadens one's understanding of the world and enhances critical thinking skills. This exchange of ideas can lead to the discovery of new interests and passions, fueling personal development and growth.

Moreover, dialogue can serve as a source of inspiration and motivation. Conversations with mentors, peers, or role models can ignite a sense of purpose and drive. Hearing about others' experiences and achievements can encourage individuals to pursue their own goals with renewed vigor. Dialogue can also provide encouragement and support during challenging times, reinforcing resilience and determination.

The transformative power of dialogue lies in its ability to facilitate change. Through conversations, individuals can explore new possibilities and envision a future that aligns with their aspirations. Dialogue encourages individuals to step outside their comfort zones, embrace new challenges, and take proactive steps towards personal development. It provides a platform for setting goals, creating action plans, and holding oneself accountable.

In addition to fostering individual growth, dialogue can also enhance interpersonal relationships. Effective communication skills, developed through dialogue, are essential for building trust and rapport with others. By engaging in open and honest conversations, individuals can strengthen their connections with family, friends, and colleagues. These relationships provide a supportive network that can contribute to personal development and well-being.

Dialogue is not limited to verbal exchanges; it also encompasses nonverbal communication. Body language, facial expressions, and tone of voice all play a role in conveying messages and emotions. Being attuned to these nonverbal cues can enhance the quality of dialogue and deepen understanding between individuals. This awareness of nonverbal communication is an important aspect of personal development, as it fosters empathy and emotional intelligence.

To harness the full potential of dialogue in personal development, it is essential to cultivate active listening skills. Active listening involves being fully present in the conversation, paying attention to the speaker's words and emotions, and responding with empathy and understanding. By practicing active listening, individuals can create a safe and supportive environment for dialogue, encouraging open and honest communication.

Another key element of effective dialogue is the ability to ask thoughtful and probing questions. Questions that encourage reflection and exploration can lead to deeper insights and understanding. By asking open-ended questions, individuals can guide conversations towards meaningful topics and facilitate self-discovery. This skill is particularly valuable in personal development, as it empowers individuals to uncover their true potential and aspirations.

# Understanding the Dynamics of Change

Change is an inevitable part of life, a constant force that shapes our experiences and molds our identities. Understanding the dynamics of change is crucial for navigating the complexities of personal and professional growth. It involves recognizing the patterns and processes that accompany change, as well as developing strategies to adapt and thrive in an ever-evolving world.

At its core, change is a transition from one state to another. This transition can be triggered by various factors, such as external events, internal realizations, or a combination of both. The dynamics of change are influenced by the interplay between these factors and the individual's response to them. By examining these dynamics, one can gain valuable insights into how change unfolds and how to harness its potential for personal development.

One of the key aspects of understanding change is recognizing its stages. Change often follows a predictable pattern, consisting of distinct phases that individuals experience as they adapt to new circumstances. These stages include denial, resistance, exploration, and acceptance. Each stage presents unique challenges and opportunities for growth, and understanding them can help individuals navigate the change process more effectively.

Denial is the initial stage of change, characterized by a reluctance to acknowledge the need for change or the reality of the situation. This stage is often marked by feelings of disbelief or avoidance, as individuals struggle to come to terms with the impending transition. Recognizing denial is the first step towards embracing change, as it allows individuals to confront their fears and begin the process of adaptation.

Resistance is a natural response to change, as individuals grapple with the uncertainty and discomfort that often accompany transitions. This stage is characterized by a desire to maintain the status quo and a reluctance to let go of familiar routines and habits. Understanding the reasons behind resistance can help individuals address their concerns and develop strategies to overcome it. This may involve seeking support from others, reframing negative thoughts, or focusing on the potential benefits of change.

Exploration is the stage where individuals begin to experiment with new ideas and behaviors, testing the waters of change. This phase is marked by curiosity and a willingness to take risks, as individuals explore different possibilities and assess their potential impact. Embracing exploration can lead to valuable insights and discoveries, as individuals learn more about themselves and their capabilities. It is during this stage that individuals can identify new opportunities for growth and development.

Acceptance is the final stage of change, where individuals come to terms with the new reality and integrate it into their lives. This stage is characterized by a sense of resolution and a commitment to moving forward. Acceptance does not mean that all challenges have been overcome, but rather that individuals have developed the resilience and adaptability needed to thrive in the face of change. By embracing acceptance, individuals can fully harness the transformative power of change and use it as a catalyst for personal growth.

In addition to understanding the stages of change, it is important to recognize the factors that influence how individuals experience and respond to change. These factors can include personality traits, past experiences, and the support systems available to individuals. By examining these influences, individuals can gain a deeper understanding of their own responses to change and develop strategies to manage them effectively.

Personality traits play a significant role in shaping how individuals perceive and respond to change. For example, individuals with a high tolerance for ambiguity may be more comfortable with uncertainty and more willing to embrace change. Conversely, those with a strong need for stability may find change more challenging and may require additional support to navigate transitions. Understanding one's personality traits can provide valuable insights into how to approach change and develop strategies to manage it effectively.

Past experiences also influence how individuals respond to change. Previous encounters with change can shape one's expectations and attitudes towards future transitions. For example, individuals who have successfully navigated change in the past may feel more confident in their ability to adapt to new circumstances. Conversely, those who have experienced negative outcomes may be more hesitant to embrace change. Reflecting on past experiences can help individuals identify patterns and develop strategies to build resilience and adaptability.

Support systems play a crucial role in helping individuals navigate change. Having a network of supportive friends, family, or colleagues can provide valuable encouragement and guidance during times of transition. These support systems can offer practical assistance, emotional support, and a sense of connection, all of which can help individuals manage the challenges of change more effectively. Building and maintaining strong support networks is an essential component of successfully navigating change.

To effectively manage change, individuals can develop a range of strategies and techniques. These may include setting clear goals, developing a flexible mindset, and practicing self-care. Setting clear goals can provide a sense of direction and purpose during times of change, helping individuals stay focused and motivated. Developing a flexible mindset involves cultivating an openness to new ideas and a willingness to adapt to changing circumstances. Practicing self-care is essential for maintaining physical and emotional well-being during times of change, as it helps individuals build resilience and cope with stress.

## The Counselor's Influence in Transformative Conversations

In the realm of transformative conversations, the counselor's influence is both profound and multifaceted. These dialogues serve as a catalyst for change, offering individuals the opportunity to explore their thoughts, emotions, and behaviors in a safe and supportive environment. The counselor, as a skilled facilitator, plays a pivotal role in guiding these conversations, helping clients uncover insights and develop strategies for personal growth.

At the heart of the counselor's influence is the ability to create a therapeutic alliance. This relationship is built on trust, empathy, and mutual respect, providing a foundation for open and honest communication. The counselor's presence and demeanor set the tone for the conversation, encouraging clients to share their experiences and express their vulnerabilities without fear of judgment. By fostering a sense of safety and acceptance, the counselor empowers clients to engage in self-exploration and reflection.

Active listening is a fundamental skill that counselors employ to influence transformative conversations. This involves fully attending to the client's words, emotions, and nonverbal cues, demonstrating genuine interest and understanding. Through active listening, counselors validate the client's experiences and feelings, reinforcing their sense of worth and importance. This validation encourages clients to delve deeper into their thoughts and emotions, facilitating greater self-awareness and insight.

The counselor's use of open-ended questions is another powerful tool in transformative conversations. These questions invite clients to explore their thoughts and feelings more thoroughly, prompting them to consider different perspectives and possibilities. By encouraging clients to articulate their experiences in their own words, counselors help them gain clarity and develop a deeper understanding of their motivations and desires. This process of self-discovery is essential for fostering change and growth.

Reflective responses are another technique counselors use to influence transformative conversations. By paraphrasing or summarizing the client's statements, counselors demonstrate their understanding and help clients gain new insights into their experiences. Reflective responses can also highlight patterns or themes in the client's narrative, encouraging them to consider how these may be influencing their current situation. This reflection can lead to a greater awareness of the underlying issues and dynamics at play, paving the way for meaningful change.

Counselors also play a crucial role in challenging clients' assumptions and beliefs. By gently questioning or reframing these beliefs, counselors encourage clients to examine their validity and consider alternative viewpoints. This process can help clients identify and overcome cognitive distortions or limiting beliefs that may be hindering their progress. By fostering a more flexible and adaptive mindset, counselors empower clients to embrace change and pursue new possibilities.

The counselor's influence extends beyond the content of the conversation to the process itself. By modeling effective communication skills, such as active listening, empathy, and assertiveness, counselors provide clients with valuable tools for navigating their own relationships and interactions. These skills can enhance clients' ability to engage in transformative conversations outside the counseling setting, promoting personal growth and development in all areas of their lives.

In addition to these interpersonal skills, counselors draw on a range of theoretical frameworks and techniques to guide transformative conversations. These may include cognitive-behavioral strategies, mindfulness practices, or narrative therapy approaches, among others. By tailoring their approach to the unique needs and goals of each client, counselors can facilitate more effective and meaningful conversations, fostering lasting change and growth.

The counselor's influence in transformative conversations is not limited to individual sessions. Group counseling and support groups also provide valuable opportunities for clients to engage in transformative dialogues. In these settings, the counselor's role is to facilitate open and respectful communication among group members, creating a supportive environment where individuals can share their experiences and learn from one another. The collective wisdom and support of the group can enhance the transformative potential of these conversations, providing clients with additional insights and perspectives.

Counselors also recognize the importance of cultural competence in transformative conversations. By understanding and respecting the diverse backgrounds and experiences of their clients, counselors can create a more inclusive and empowering environment. This involves being aware of cultural differences in communication styles, values, and beliefs, and adapting their approach accordingly. By honoring the client's cultural identity, counselors can foster a deeper sense of connection and trust, enhancing the effectiveness of the conversation.

The counselor's influence in transformative conversations is ultimately about empowering clients to take ownership of their own growth and development. By providing a supportive and nonjudgmental space for exploration and reflection, counselors help clients identify their strengths, values, and goals. This process of self-discovery enables clients to develop a clearer sense of purpose and direction, motivating them to take action and make positive changes in their lives.

## Setting the Stage for Lasting Impact

Creating a foundation for lasting impact requires a thoughtful approach, one that considers both the immediate and long-term effects of actions and decisions. The process begins with a clear understanding of the desired outcomes and the factors that contribute to achieving them. This involves setting specific, measurable goals that align with a broader vision, ensuring that every step taken is purposeful and directed towards meaningful change.

A crucial element in setting the stage for lasting impact is the identification and engagement of key stakeholders. These individuals or groups have a vested interest in the outcomes and can significantly influence the success of any initiative. By involving stakeholders early in the process, their insights and perspectives can be integrated into the planning and execution phases, fostering a sense of ownership and commitment. This collaborative approach not only enhances the quality of the outcomes but also builds a network of support that can sustain efforts over time.

Effective communication is another cornerstone of creating lasting impact. Clear, consistent messaging helps to articulate the vision and goals, ensuring that all parties involved understand their roles and responsibilities. This transparency fosters trust and accountability, essential components for maintaining momentum and achieving long-term success. Additionally, open channels of communication allow for the exchange of ideas and feedback, enabling continuous improvement and adaptation to changing circumstances.

The allocation of resources is a critical consideration in setting the stage for lasting impact. This includes not only financial resources but also human capital, time, and technology. Strategic resource management ensures that efforts are focused and efficient, maximizing the potential for positive outcomes. It is important to prioritize initiatives that align with the overarching goals and to be flexible in reallocating resources as needed to address emerging challenges or opportunities.

Building capacity within the organization or community is another key factor in achieving lasting impact. This involves developing the skills, knowledge, and abilities of individuals and teams to effectively implement and sustain initiatives. Capacity building can take many forms, including training programs, mentorship, and the establishment of supportive networks. By empowering individuals with the tools and resources they need to succeed, the likelihood of achieving and maintaining positive change is greatly increased.

Monitoring and evaluation play a vital role in ensuring that efforts lead to lasting impact. By establishing metrics and benchmarks, progress can be tracked and assessed over time. This data-driven approach allows for the identification of successes and areas for improvement, informing decision-making and guiding future actions. Regular evaluation also provides an opportunity to celebrate achievements and recognize the contributions of those involved, reinforcing commitment and motivation.

Adaptability is essential in the pursuit of lasting impact. The ability to respond to changing circumstances and to learn from both successes and failures is crucial for sustained progress. This requires a mindset that embraces innovation and experimentation, encouraging the exploration of new ideas and approaches. By remaining open to change and willing to adjust strategies as needed, the potential for achieving meaningful and enduring outcomes is significantly enhanced.

Sustainability is a fundamental consideration in setting the stage for lasting impact. This involves ensuring that initiatives are designed to endure beyond their initial implementation, with mechanisms in place to support ongoing efforts. This may include the establishment of policies, systems, and structures that institutionalize change, as well as the cultivation of partnerships and alliances that provide ongoing support and resources. By embedding sustainability into the fabric of initiatives, the likelihood of achieving long-term success is greatly increased.

The role of leadership in creating lasting impact cannot be overstated. Effective leaders inspire and motivate others, setting a positive example and fostering a culture of collaboration and innovation. They are adept at navigating complex challenges and making informed decisions that align with the overarching vision and goals. By cultivating strong leadership at all levels, organizations and communities are better equipped to achieve and sustain meaningful change.

Finally, the importance of reflection and learning in the pursuit of lasting impact should not be overlooked. Taking the time to reflect on experiences, both individually and collectively, provides valuable insights and lessons that can inform future efforts. This reflective practice encourages a culture of continuous learning and improvement, fostering resilience and adaptability in the face of challenges.

# Chapter 2

# Foundations of Effective Communication

## The Art of Active Listening

Active listening is a skill that transcends mere hearing, transforming communication into a powerful tool for connection and understanding. It involves fully engaging with the speaker, not just with the ears, but with the mind and heart as well. This art requires patience, empathy, and a genuine interest in the other person's perspective, creating an environment where meaningful dialogue can flourish.

The foundation of active listening lies in the ability to focus entirely on the speaker. This means setting aside distractions, both external and internal, to give undivided attention. In a world filled with constant noise and interruptions, this can be challenging, yet it is essential for truly understanding the message being conveyed. By being present in the moment, the listener can pick up on subtle cues and nuances that might otherwise be missed.

Nonverbal communication plays a significant role in active listening. Body language, facial expressions, and eye contact all contribute to the listener's engagement with the speaker. Maintaining an open and receptive posture signals interest and attentiveness, encouraging the speaker to share more openly. A nod of the head or a warm smile can convey understanding and empathy, reinforcing the connection between the speaker and listener.

Reflective listening is a technique that enhances active listening by allowing the listener to paraphrase or summarize what the speaker has said. This not only demonstrates that the listener is paying attention but also provides an opportunity for clarification. By reflecting back the speaker's words, the listener can confirm their understanding and ensure that the message has been accurately received. This process fosters a sense of validation and respect, encouraging further dialogue.

Empathy is a cornerstone of active listening, enabling the listener to connect with the speaker on an emotional level. By putting oneself in the speaker's shoes, the listener can better understand their feelings and perspectives. This empathetic approach helps to build trust and rapport, creating a safe space for open and honest communication. It also allows the listener to respond with sensitivity and compassion, addressing the speaker's needs and concerns.

Asking open-ended questions is another effective strategy in active listening. These questions invite the speaker to elaborate on their thoughts and feelings, providing deeper insights into their perspective. By encouraging the speaker to share more, the listener can gain a more comprehensive understanding of the situation. This approach also demonstrates genuine interest and curiosity, reinforcing the speaker's sense of being heard and valued.

Active listening requires the listener to manage their own biases and assumptions. Preconceived notions can cloud judgment and hinder the ability to truly understand the speaker's message. By approaching each conversation with an open mind and a willingness to learn, the listener can overcome these barriers and engage in more meaningful dialogue. This openness fosters a culture of mutual respect and understanding, where diverse perspectives are welcomed and appreciated.

Silence is a powerful tool in active listening, providing space for reflection and contemplation. Allowing moments of silence during a conversation gives the speaker time to gather their thoughts and express themselves more fully. It also allows the listener to process the information and formulate thoughtful responses. Embracing silence as a natural part of communication can lead to deeper insights and more profound connections.

Feedback is an essential component of active listening, offering the speaker reassurance that their message has been received and understood. Constructive feedback should be delivered with care and consideration, focusing on the content of the message rather than the speaker themselves. By providing feedback that is specific and relevant, the listener can contribute to a more productive and collaborative conversation.

The practice of active listening extends beyond individual interactions, influencing the dynamics of teams and organizations. In a professional setting, active listening can enhance collaboration, foster innovation, and improve decision-making. By creating an environment where all voices are heard and valued, organizations can harness the collective wisdom of their members to achieve shared goals.

Active listening also plays a vital role in conflict resolution, helping to bridge gaps and find common ground. By listening with empathy and understanding, parties in conflict can move beyond their differences and work towards mutually beneficial solutions. This approach fosters a spirit of cooperation and compromise, reducing tension and promoting harmony.

In personal relationships, active listening strengthens bonds and deepens connections. By truly hearing and understanding one another, individuals can build trust and intimacy, creating a foundation for lasting and meaningful relationships. This skill enhances communication and reduces misunderstandings, paving the way for more fulfilling interactions.

Developing the art of active listening requires practice and dedication. It involves a commitment to being present, empathetic, and open-minded in every interaction. By honing this skill, individuals can transform their communication and enrich their relationships, both personally and professionally.

## Building Trust and Rapport

Trust and rapport are the cornerstones of any meaningful relationship, whether personal or professional. They form the bedrock upon which successful interactions are built, fostering an environment of mutual respect and understanding. Establishing trust and rapport requires intentional effort and a genuine commitment to nurturing connections with others.

The journey to building trust begins with authenticity. Being genuine and transparent in your interactions allows others to see the real you, fostering a sense of reliability and dependability. People are more likely to trust those who are consistent in their words and actions, as this consistency signals integrity and honesty. By being true to yourself and your values, you create a foundation of trust that others can rely on.

Active listening is a powerful tool in building rapport. By fully engaging with the speaker and demonstrating genuine interest in their perspective, you show that you value their thoughts and feelings. This attentiveness fosters a sense of connection and understanding, encouraging open and honest communication. When people feel heard and understood, they are more likely to reciprocate with trust and openness.

Empathy plays a crucial role in establishing trust and rapport. By putting yourself in the other person's shoes and understanding their emotions and experiences, you demonstrate compassion and sensitivity. This empathetic approach helps to build a bridge between individuals, creating a safe space for vulnerability and authenticity. When people feel that their emotions are acknowledged and respected, they are more likely to trust and open up.

Consistency in behavior and communication is essential for building trust. People need to know that they can rely on you to act in a predictable and dependable manner. This means following through on promises, meeting commitments, and being accountable for your actions. By consistently demonstrating reliability, you reinforce the trust that others have placed in you, strengthening the bond of rapport.

Honesty is a fundamental component of trust. Being truthful in your interactions, even when it is difficult, shows that you respect the other person and value the relationship. Honesty fosters transparency and openness, allowing for more authentic and meaningful connections. When people know that they can count on you to be truthful, they are more likely to trust you and engage in open dialogue.

Building rapport involves finding common ground and shared interests. By identifying areas of mutual interest or experience, you create a sense of camaraderie and connection. This shared understanding fosters a sense of belonging and acceptance, encouraging more open and honest communication. When people feel that they have something in common with you, they are more likely to trust and engage with you.

Nonverbal communication is a powerful tool in building trust and rapport. Body language, facial expressions, and eye contact all convey messages of interest and engagement. By maintaining an open and receptive posture, you signal that you are approachable and willing to connect. A warm smile or a nod of the head can convey understanding and empathy, reinforcing the bond of rapport.

Trust is built over time through consistent and positive interactions. It requires patience and perseverance, as trust cannot be rushed or forced. By investing time and effort into nurturing relationships, you create a foundation of trust that can withstand challenges and adversity. This long-term commitment to building trust and rapport pays dividends in the form of deeper and more meaningful connections.

In professional settings, trust and rapport are essential for effective teamwork and collaboration. When team members trust one another, they are more likely to share ideas, take risks, and work together towards common goals. This collaborative environment fosters innovation and creativity, driving success and achievement. By building trust and rapport within a team, you create a culture of mutual respect and support, where all members feel valued and empowered.

In personal relationships, trust and rapport are the glue that holds connections together. They allow individuals to be vulnerable and authentic, creating a safe space for intimacy and closeness. By nurturing trust and rapport, you strengthen the bonds of friendship and love, creating lasting and fulfilling relationships.

Conflict resolution is another area where trust and rapport play a vital role. When individuals trust one another, they are more likely to approach conflicts with a spirit of cooperation and compromise. This trust allows for open and honest communication, where all parties feel heard and respected. By building rapport, you create an environment where conflicts can be resolved constructively, leading to mutually beneficial outcomes.

Developing trust and rapport requires self-awareness and emotional intelligence. It involves understanding your own emotions and behaviors, as well as those of others. By being mindful of your impact on others and adjusting your approach accordingly, you can build stronger and more meaningful connections. This self-awareness allows you to navigate complex social dynamics with grace and empathy, fostering trust and rapport in all your interactions.

## Nonverbal Communication Reading Between the Lines

Nonverbal communication is an intricate dance of gestures, expressions, and postures that conveys meaning beyond words. It is the silent language that speaks volumes, often revealing more than spoken dialogue ever could. Understanding and interpreting these cues can enhance interactions, providing insights into emotions, intentions, and unspoken thoughts.

The human face is a canvas of expression, capable of conveying a myriad of emotions with subtle shifts in muscle movement. A smile can signal warmth and friendliness, while a furrowed brow may indicate confusion or concern. The eyes, often referred to as the windows to the soul, can express a range of feelings from joy to sadness, or even deceit. Eye contact, in particular, plays a crucial role in communication, as it can convey confidence, interest, or aggression. The duration and intensity of eye contact can vary across cultures, making it essential to consider cultural context when interpreting these cues.

Gestures are another vital component of nonverbal communication. They can emphasize a point, illustrate a concept, or replace words altogether. A wave of the hand can signal greeting or farewell, while a thumbs-up may indicate approval or agreement. However, gestures can also be ambiguous, with meanings that differ across cultures. For instance, a gesture that is considered positive in one culture may be offensive in another. Understanding these cultural nuances is crucial for effective communication, especially in diverse or international settings.

Posture and body orientation provide additional layers of meaning in nonverbal communication. An open posture, with arms uncrossed and body facing the speaker, can indicate receptiveness and engagement. Conversely, a closed posture, with arms crossed and body turned away, may suggest defensiveness or disinterest. The way individuals position themselves in relation to others can also convey power dynamics or social status. For example, standing tall with shoulders back can project confidence and authority, while slouching may suggest insecurity or submission.

Proxemics, the study of personal space, is another critical aspect of nonverbal communication. The distance individuals maintain between themselves and others can convey intimacy, aggression, or formality. Personal space preferences can vary widely across cultures and individuals, making it essential to be attuned to these differences. Invading someone's personal space can lead to discomfort or tension, while maintaining an appropriate distance can foster a sense of respect and comfort.

Touch is a powerful form of nonverbal communication that can convey a range of emotions, from affection to aggression. A handshake can signal professionalism and respect, while a pat on the back may indicate encouragement or camaraderie. However, the appropriateness of touch can vary based on cultural norms, personal preferences, and the nature of the relationship. Being mindful of these factors is crucial to avoid misunderstandings or discomfort.

Paralanguage, the vocal elements that accompany speech, adds another dimension to nonverbal communication. Tone, pitch, volume, and rhythm can all influence the meaning of spoken words. A soft, gentle tone may convey warmth and empathy, while a loud, harsh tone may suggest anger or frustration. The way words are delivered can significantly impact how they are perceived, making it essential to be aware of these vocal cues.

Microexpressions, fleeting facial expressions that occur involuntarily, can reveal genuine emotions that individuals may attempt to conceal. These brief expressions, often lasting only a fraction of a second, can provide valuable insights into a person's true feelings. Detecting and interpreting microexpressions requires keen observation and practice, but mastering this skill can enhance one's ability to read between the lines.

Cultural context plays a significant role in nonverbal communication, as gestures, expressions, and behaviors can have different meanings across cultures. What is considered polite or respectful in one culture may be perceived as rude or inappropriate in another. Being aware of these cultural differences and adapting one's communication style accordingly is essential for effective cross-cultural interactions.

Nonverbal communication is not only about interpreting others' cues but also about being aware of one's own signals. Self-awareness and self-regulation are crucial for ensuring that nonverbal cues align with verbal messages. Inconsistencies between verbal and nonverbal communication can lead to confusion or mistrust, as people tend to rely more on nonverbal cues when interpreting messages.

Developing the ability to read nonverbal cues requires practice and observation. Paying attention to the context, the individual's baseline behavior, and any deviations from that baseline can provide valuable insights. It is also essential to consider the congruence between verbal and nonverbal messages, as discrepancies may indicate deception or discomfort.

In professional settings, nonverbal communication can influence perceptions of competence, confidence, and credibility. A firm handshake, steady eye contact, and confident posture can enhance one's professional image, while nervous gestures or lack of eye contact may undermine it. Being mindful of nonverbal cues can enhance presentations, negotiations, and interpersonal interactions, contributing to professional success.

In personal relationships, nonverbal communication can deepen connections and foster intimacy. Understanding a partner's nonverbal cues can enhance empathy and emotional attunement, leading to more meaningful and fulfilling relationships. Being attuned to nonverbal signals can also help navigate conflicts, as it allows individuals to address underlying emotions and concerns.

## The Power of Empathy in Dialogue

Empathy, the ability to understand and share the feelings of another, is a transformative force in dialogue. It bridges gaps, fosters connection, and creates an environment where open communication can flourish. In a world where misunderstandings and conflicts are commonplace, empathy serves as a vital tool for navigating conversations with grace and understanding.

Imagine a conversation between two individuals with differing viewpoints. Without empathy, this exchange might quickly devolve into a heated argument, with each party entrenched in their own perspective. However, when empathy is present, the dynamic shifts. Each person becomes more willing to listen, to consider the other's feelings and experiences, and to find common ground. This shift can lead to more productive and meaningful dialogues, where both parties feel heard and respected.

Empathy begins with active listening, a skill that requires full attention and presence. It involves not only hearing the words being spoken but also paying attention to the speaker's tone, body language, and emotional cues. By focusing on the speaker and setting aside distractions, one can better understand the underlying emotions and intentions behind their words. This understanding is crucial for responding in a way that acknowledges and validates the speaker's feelings.

Reflective listening is another powerful technique that enhances empathy in dialogue. By paraphrasing or summarizing what the speaker has said, the listener demonstrates that they have truly heard and understood the message. This not only reassures the speaker but also provides an opportunity for clarification if any misunderstandings arise. Reflective listening fosters a sense of collaboration and mutual respect, as both parties work together to ensure clear and effective communication.

Empathy also involves putting oneself in another's shoes, imagining how they might feel in a given situation. This perspective-taking can be challenging, especially when one's own emotions or biases come into play. However, by consciously setting aside personal judgments and focusing on the other person's experience, one can gain a deeper understanding of their perspective. This understanding can lead to more compassionate and empathetic responses, which can defuse tension and build rapport.

Incorporating empathy into dialogue requires self-awareness and emotional intelligence. Recognizing one's own emotions and triggers is essential for maintaining composure and responding empathetically, even in challenging situations. By managing one's emotions and remaining calm, one can create a safe space for open and honest communication. This emotional regulation is particularly important in high-stakes or emotionally charged conversations, where empathy can prevent escalation and promote resolution.

Empathy is not only about understanding others but also about expressing one's own feelings and needs in a way that invites empathy in return. Using "I" statements, such as "I feel" or "I need," can help convey emotions without placing blame or making accusations. This approach encourages the other person to respond with empathy, as it focuses on personal experiences rather than assigning fault. By modeling empathetic communication, one can inspire others to do the same, creating a positive feedback loop of understanding and connection.

In professional settings, empathy can enhance teamwork, collaboration, and leadership. Leaders who demonstrate empathy are more likely to build trust and loyalty among their team members, as they create an environment where individuals feel valued and supported. Empathetic leaders are also better equipped to navigate conflicts, as they can address underlying emotions and concerns with sensitivity and care. By fostering a culture of empathy, organizations can improve morale, productivity, and overall success.

In personal relationships, empathy is the cornerstone of intimacy and connection. It allows individuals to truly see and understand one another, fostering a sense of closeness and trust. Empathy can also help navigate disagreements or misunderstandings, as it encourages open communication and mutual respect.

By prioritizing empathy in relationships, individuals can build stronger, more fulfilling connections with their loved ones.

Empathy is a skill that can be cultivated and strengthened over time. Practicing mindfulness and self-reflection can enhance one's ability to empathize, as it encourages greater awareness of one's own emotions and those of others. Engaging in activities that promote empathy, such as volunteering or reading literature that explores diverse perspectives, can also broaden one's understanding and appreciation of different experiences.

## Overcoming Barriers to Effective Communication

Effective communication is an essential skill that underpins successful interactions in both personal and professional settings. Yet, numerous barriers can impede the flow of clear and meaningful dialogue. These obstacles, whether rooted in language, cultural differences, or personal biases, can lead to misunderstandings and conflict. Understanding and overcoming these barriers is crucial for fostering open and productive communication.

One of the most common barriers is language. Even when individuals speak the same language, differences in vocabulary, dialects, or jargon can create confusion. This is particularly evident in professional environments where industry-specific terminology may be unfamiliar to those outside the field. To mitigate this barrier, it's important to use clear and simple language, avoiding technical terms unless they are necessary and well-explained. When communicating with someone who speaks a different language, using visual aids or translation tools can help bridge the gap and ensure mutual understanding.

Cultural differences also play a significant role in communication barriers. Each culture has its own set of norms, values, and communication styles, which can lead to misunderstandings when individuals from different backgrounds interact. For example, some cultures may prioritize directness and assertiveness, while others value indirect communication and harmony. Being aware of these cultural nuances and approaching interactions with an open mind can help navigate these differences. Taking the time to learn about and respect other cultures can enhance cross-cultural communication and build stronger relationships.

Personal biases and assumptions can also hinder effective communication. These biases, often unconscious, can lead individuals to make judgments or assumptions about others based on stereotypes or preconceived notions. Such biases can affect how messages are sent, received, and interpreted, leading to miscommunication. To overcome this barrier, it's important to cultivate self-awareness and challenge one's own assumptions. Engaging in active listening and seeking to understand the other person's perspective can help counteract biases and foster more open and honest communication.

Emotional barriers, such as stress, anxiety, or anger, can also impede effective communication. When emotions run high, individuals may struggle to articulate their thoughts clearly or may misinterpret the messages of others. Managing emotions and maintaining composure is essential for clear communication. Techniques such as deep breathing, mindfulness, or taking a moment to pause before responding can help regulate emotions and create a more conducive environment for dialogue.

Physical barriers, such as noise, distance, or technological issues, can also disrupt communication. In today's digital age, virtual communication has become increasingly common, but it comes with its own set of challenges. Technical glitches, poor internet connections, or lack of non-verbal cues can hinder the flow of conversation. To address these barriers, it's important to ensure that the communication environment is as distraction-free as possible. Using reliable technology, testing equipment beforehand, and being mindful of time zones and cultural differences in virtual meetings can enhance the effectiveness of digital communication.

Listening is a fundamental component of effective communication, yet it is often overlooked. Many individuals focus on speaking rather than truly listening to the other person. Active listening involves giving full attention to the speaker, acknowledging their message, and responding thoughtfully. This requires setting aside distractions, such as phones or other devices, and being present in the moment. By practicing active listening, individuals can better understand the speaker's perspective and respond in a way that fosters mutual respect and understanding.

Feedback is another crucial aspect of overcoming communication barriers. Providing and receiving feedback helps clarify messages, address misunderstandings, and improve future interactions. Constructive feedback should be specific, focused on behavior rather than personal attributes, and delivered in a respectful manner. Encouraging open dialogue and creating a safe space for feedback can enhance communication and strengthen relationships.

Non-verbal communication, such as body language, facial expressions, and tone of voice, plays a significant role in conveying messages. In some cases, non-verbal cues can contradict verbal messages, leading to confusion. Being aware of one's own non-verbal signals and interpreting those of others can enhance understanding and prevent miscommunication. In virtual settings, where non-verbal cues may be limited, paying attention to tone of voice and using clear and expressive language can help convey messages effectively.

Building trust is essential for overcoming communication barriers. Trust creates a foundation for open and honest dialogue, where individuals feel comfortable expressing their thoughts and feelings. Building trust requires consistency, transparency, and integrity in communication. By demonstrating reliability and authenticity, individuals can foster trust and create an environment where effective communication can thrive.

Empathy is a powerful tool for overcoming communication barriers. By putting oneself in another's shoes and seeking to understand their feelings and experiences, individuals can bridge gaps and foster connection. Empathy involves active listening, perspective-taking, and responding with compassion and understanding. By prioritizing empathy in communication, individuals can navigate differences and build stronger, more meaningful relationships.

# Chapter 3

# Crafting Empowering Conversations

## Techniques for Encouraging Openness

Openness in communication is a cornerstone of healthy relationships, whether personal or professional. It fosters trust, understanding, and collaboration, allowing individuals to express themselves freely and authentically. However, encouraging openness can be challenging, especially in environments where individuals may feel hesitant or guarded. Employing effective techniques can help create a space where openness thrives, leading to more meaningful and productive interactions.

Creating a safe and supportive environment is fundamental to encouraging openness. Individuals are more likely to share their thoughts and feelings when they feel secure and respected. Establishing ground rules for communication, such as active listening and non-judgmental responses, can help create a foundation of trust. It's important to demonstrate empathy and understanding, acknowledging the other person's perspective without immediately offering solutions or judgments. By showing genuine interest and concern, individuals can foster a sense of safety that encourages openness.

Active listening is a powerful tool for promoting openness. It involves fully engaging with the speaker, giving them undivided attention, and responding thoughtfully. This means setting aside distractions, such as phones or other devices, and being present in the moment. Reflective listening, where the listener paraphrases or summarizes what the speaker has said, can help clarify messages and demonstrate understanding. By practicing active listening, individuals can create an environment where others feel heard and valued, encouraging them to share more openly.

Asking open-ended questions is another effective technique for encouraging openness. Unlike closed questions that elicit a simple yes or no response, open-ended questions invite the speaker to elaborate and share more details. These questions often begin with words like "how," "what," or "why," prompting deeper reflection and discussion. For example, instead of asking, "Did you like the presentation?" one might ask, "What aspects of the presentation resonated with you?" This approach encourages the speaker to explore their thoughts and feelings more fully, leading to richer and more open communication.

Modeling openness is a powerful way to encourage others to be open. When individuals demonstrate vulnerability and authenticity in their own communication, it sets a precedent for others to follow. Sharing personal experiences, admitting mistakes, or expressing emotions can create a sense of relatability and trust. By being open themselves, individuals signal that it is safe for others to do the same, fostering an environment where openness is valued and encouraged.

Building rapport and establishing a connection with others can also promote openness. Taking the time to get to know the other person, understanding their interests, and finding common ground can create a sense of camaraderie and trust. This can be achieved through informal conversations, shared activities, or simply expressing genuine interest in the other person's life. By building rapport, individuals can create a foundation of trust that encourages open and honest communication.

Providing positive reinforcement and feedback can also encourage openness. Acknowledging and appreciating the other person's contributions, even if they are small, can boost their confidence and willingness to share. Constructive feedback should be specific, focused on behavior rather than personal attributes, and delivered in a respectful manner. By creating a positive and supportive atmosphere, individuals can encourage others to express themselves more openly and confidently.

Creating opportunities for open dialogue is essential for encouraging openness. This can be achieved through regular check-ins, team meetings, or one-on-one conversations. Providing a platform for individuals to share their thoughts, ideas, and concerns can foster a culture of openness and collaboration. It's important to ensure that these opportunities are inclusive and accessible to all, allowing everyone to participate and contribute.

Addressing and managing conflict is crucial for maintaining openness. Conflict can create tension and hinder open communication, but it can also be an opportunity for growth and understanding.

Approaching conflict with a mindset of curiosity and empathy, rather than defensiveness or blame, can help resolve issues and promote openness. Encouraging open and honest dialogue, where individuals feel safe to express their concerns and emotions, can lead to more constructive and collaborative outcomes.

Encouraging openness requires a commitment to continuous learning and growth. This means being open to feedback, reflecting on one's own communication style, and seeking opportunities for improvement. By embracing a growth mindset, individuals can adapt and evolve their communication techniques, fostering a culture of openness and collaboration.

## Asking the Right Questions

The art of asking the right questions is a skill that can transform conversations, uncover hidden insights, and foster deeper connections. Whether in personal interactions, professional settings, or academic pursuits, the ability to pose thoughtful and effective questions can lead to more meaningful and productive exchanges. Understanding the nuances of questioning can empower individuals to navigate complex situations, solve problems, and engage others in a more profound way.

At the heart of effective questioning lies the distinction between open-ended and closed questions. Open-ended questions invite expansive responses, encouraging the speaker to elaborate and explore their thoughts and feelings. These questions often begin with words like "how," "what," or "why," and they create space for dialogue and discovery. For instance, asking "What inspired you to pursue this project?" allows the respondent to share their motivations and experiences, leading to a richer understanding. In contrast, closed questions typically elicit a simple yes or no answer, limiting the depth of the conversation. While closed questions have their place, particularly when seeking specific information, open-ended questions are more conducive to fostering openness and engagement.

The context and purpose of the conversation play a crucial role in determining the types of questions to ask. In a professional setting, for example, questions might be geared towards problem-solving, decision-making, or gathering information. In such cases, clarifying questions can be particularly useful. These questions seek to confirm understanding and ensure that all parties are on the same page. For example, "Can you clarify what you mean by 'improved efficiency'?" helps to eliminate ambiguity and align expectations. In personal interactions, questions might focus on building rapport, understanding emotions, or exploring personal experiences. Here, empathetic questions that demonstrate genuine interest and concern can strengthen relationships and foster trust.

Timing and tone are also critical factors in effective questioning. The timing of a question can influence the flow of the conversation and the willingness of the respondent to engage. Asking a question too early in a discussion might catch the speaker off guard, while waiting too long might result in missed opportunities for exploration. Similarly, the tone of a question can convey curiosity, skepticism, support, or judgment. A supportive and non-judgmental tone encourages openness and honesty, while a confrontational or accusatory tone may lead to defensiveness and resistance. Being mindful of timing and tone can enhance the effectiveness of questions and create a more conducive environment for dialogue.

Active listening is an essential complement to asking the right questions. It involves fully engaging with the speaker, paying attention to their words, tone, and body language, and responding thoughtfully. By practicing active listening, individuals can identify cues and signals that inform the types of questions to ask. For example, if a speaker hesitates or seems uncertain, a follow-up question like "Can you tell me more about that?" can encourage them to elaborate and clarify their thoughts. Active listening also demonstrates respect and validation, reinforcing the speaker's willingness to share and engage.

The power of questions extends beyond verbal communication. In written communication, such as emails, reports, or surveys, crafting effective questions can elicit valuable insights and feedback. In these contexts, clarity and precision are paramount. Ambiguous or poorly worded questions can lead to confusion and misinterpretation, resulting in incomplete or inaccurate responses. Taking the time to carefully construct questions, considering the audience and the desired outcome, can enhance the quality of written communication and ensure that the information gathered is relevant and actionable.

In educational settings, asking the right questions can stimulate critical thinking, creativity, and engagement among learners. Educators can use questions to challenge assumptions, encourage exploration, and facilitate deeper understanding. For example, instead of asking students to recall facts, an educator might pose a question that requires analysis or synthesis, such as "How might this historical event have unfolded differently if certain factors had changed?" Such questions encourage learners to think critically and explore multiple perspectives, fostering a more dynamic and interactive learning experience.

In leadership and management, the ability to ask the right questions is a valuable asset. Leaders who ask insightful questions can inspire innovation, drive performance, and build cohesive teams. By encouraging open dialogue and soliciting input from team members, leaders can tap into diverse perspectives and uncover new ideas. Questions that challenge the status quo, such as "What assumptions are we making?" or "How can we approach this problem differently?" can spark creativity and drive positive change. Moreover, by asking questions that empower and engage team members, leaders can foster a culture of collaboration and continuous improvement.

The art of questioning is not limited to formal interactions; it is equally relevant in everyday life. Whether navigating personal relationships, making decisions, or seeking self-improvement, asking the right questions can lead to greater clarity and insight. Reflective questions, such as "What do I truly value?" or "How can I grow from this experience?" can promote self-awareness and personal growth. By cultivating a habit of thoughtful questioning, individuals can enhance their understanding of themselves and the world around them.

## Balancing Guidance and Autonomy

Navigating the delicate balance between guidance and autonomy is a nuanced endeavor, one that requires a keen understanding of individual needs, situational dynamics, and the overarching goals at play. This balance is particularly relevant in contexts such as education, leadership, and personal development, where the interplay between external direction and self-directed action can significantly impact outcomes. Striking the right balance can empower individuals to grow, innovate, and achieve their potential while ensuring they have the necessary support and structure to succeed.

In educational settings, the balance between guidance and autonomy is crucial for fostering an environment where students can thrive. Educators often grapple with the challenge of providing enough direction to ensure that students grasp fundamental concepts while allowing them the freedom to explore and apply their knowledge creatively. One effective approach is to adopt a scaffolded learning model, where guidance is gradually reduced as students gain confidence and competence. This method involves initially providing clear instructions and support, then progressively encouraging students to take more responsibility for their learning. By doing so, educators can cultivate independent thinkers who are capable of critical analysis and problem-solving.

The role of feedback in education is another critical component of balancing guidance and autonomy. Constructive feedback serves as a form of guidance that helps students understand their strengths and areas for improvement. However, it is essential to deliver feedback in a way that encourages self-reflection and self-assessment. Instead of simply correcting errors, educators can pose questions that prompt students to evaluate their work and consider alternative approaches. This strategy not only reinforces learning but also empowers students to take ownership of their educational journey.

In the realm of leadership, balancing guidance and autonomy is equally vital. Effective leaders recognize that micromanagement can stifle creativity and hinder team performance, while a lack of direction can lead to confusion and inefficiency. To achieve the right balance, leaders must cultivate a culture of trust and open communication. By clearly articulating goals and expectations, leaders provide the necessary framework within which team members can operate autonomously. At the same time, leaders should be available to offer support and guidance when needed, ensuring that team members feel empowered to make decisions and take initiative.

Delegation is a key aspect of leadership that exemplifies the balance between guidance and autonomy. When leaders delegate tasks, they entrust team members with the responsibility to execute those tasks independently. However, effective delegation involves more than simply assigning duties; it requires providing the necessary resources, information, and support to enable success. By setting clear objectives and boundaries, leaders can empower their teams to innovate and excel while maintaining alignment with organizational goals.

In personal development, the balance between guidance and autonomy is a deeply personal journey. Individuals often seek guidance from mentors, coaches, or self-help resources to gain insights and direction. However, true growth occurs when individuals take the initiative to apply what they have learned and chart their own path. This process involves setting personal goals, reflecting on experiences, and making informed decisions based on one's values and aspirations. By embracing autonomy, individuals can cultivate a sense of agency and self-efficacy, which are essential for personal fulfillment and success.

The concept of self-directed learning exemplifies the balance between guidance and autonomy in personal development. Self-directed learners take charge of their educational pursuits, identifying their learning needs, setting goals, and seeking resources to achieve those goals. While they may seek guidance from experts or peers, they ultimately take responsibility for their learning journey. This approach fosters a lifelong learning mindset, enabling individuals to adapt and thrive in an ever-changing world.

In professional development, the balance between guidance and autonomy can influence career progression and job satisfaction. Employees who are given the autonomy to explore new ideas and take on challenging projects often experience greater job satisfaction and motivation. However, this autonomy must be supported by a framework of guidance that includes mentorship, training, and constructive feedback. By providing opportunities for skill development and career advancement, organizations can create an environment where employees feel valued and empowered to contribute to their fullest potential.

The balance between guidance and autonomy is not static; it evolves over time and varies across different contexts and individuals. Factors such as experience, confidence, and the complexity of the task at hand can influence the level of guidance or autonomy required. For instance, a novice may need more structured guidance to build foundational skills, while an experienced professional may thrive with greater autonomy to innovate and lead. Recognizing and adapting to these nuances is essential for achieving the optimal balance.

## Navigating Difficult Topics with Sensitivity

Addressing difficult topics requires a delicate balance of empathy, understanding, and effective communication. Whether in personal conversations, educational settings, or professional environments, the ability to navigate sensitive subjects with care is essential for fostering trust, promoting open dialogue, and achieving meaningful outcomes. This chapter delves into strategies and considerations for approaching challenging discussions with sensitivity and respect.

One of the foundational elements of navigating difficult topics is active listening. This involves more than simply hearing the words being spoken; it requires a genuine effort to understand the speaker's perspective, emotions, and underlying concerns. Active listening demonstrates respect and empathy, creating a safe space for individuals to express themselves without fear of judgment or dismissal. By focusing on the speaker and providing verbal and non-verbal cues of attentiveness, such as nodding or maintaining eye contact, listeners can convey their commitment to understanding and valuing the speaker's viewpoint.

Empathy plays a crucial role in addressing sensitive subjects. It involves putting oneself in another's shoes and acknowledging their feelings and experiences. Empathy fosters connection and trust, allowing individuals to feel heard and validated. When discussing difficult topics, expressing empathy can help diffuse tension and create an atmosphere of mutual respect. Phrases such as "I can imagine how that must feel" or "It sounds like you're going through a lot" can convey empathy and encourage open communication.

Another important aspect of navigating difficult topics is the use of inclusive language. Language has the power to shape perceptions and influence emotions, so it is essential to choose words carefully. Inclusive language avoids assumptions and stereotypes, promoting a sense of belonging and respect for all individuals involved in the conversation. For example, using gender-neutral terms or avoiding labels that may carry negative connotations can help create an inclusive environment. Additionally, being mindful of cultural differences and sensitivities can prevent misunderstandings and foster a more respectful dialogue.

Timing and context are also critical factors to consider when addressing sensitive subjects. Choosing an appropriate time and setting for the conversation can significantly impact its outcome. It is important to ensure that all parties involved are in a conducive state of mind and that the environment is private and free from distractions. This consideration demonstrates respect for the gravity of the topic and the individuals involved. Additionally, being aware of the emotional state of the participants can help determine the right moment to broach the subject, as emotions can influence the receptiveness and effectiveness of the discussion.

When engaging in conversations about difficult topics, it is essential to remain open-minded and non-judgmental. Preconceived notions and biases can hinder effective communication and prevent a genuine understanding of the other person's perspective. Approaching the conversation with curiosity and a willingness to learn can lead to more productive and meaningful exchanges. Asking open-ended questions and encouraging the speaker to elaborate on their thoughts and feelings can provide valuable insights and facilitate a deeper understanding of the issue at hand.

Setting clear intentions and goals for the conversation can also enhance its effectiveness. Before initiating a discussion on a sensitive topic, it is helpful to clarify the purpose and desired outcome of the conversation.

This clarity can guide the direction of the dialogue and ensure that all parties are aligned in their objectives. Whether the goal is to resolve a conflict, gain a better understanding of a differing viewpoint, or provide support, having a clear intention can help maintain focus and prevent the conversation from veering off course.

In situations where emotions run high, it is important to manage emotional responses constructively. Emotions are a natural part of difficult conversations, but they can sometimes escalate and hinder effective communication. Recognizing and acknowledging emotions, both one's own and those of others, can help manage them more effectively. Techniques such as deep breathing, taking a moment to pause, or using "I" statements to express feelings can help regulate emotions and maintain a calm and respectful dialogue.

It is also important to recognize when a conversation may need to be paused or revisited at a later time. If emotions become overwhelming or if the discussion reaches an impasse, it may be beneficial to take a break and allow all parties to reflect and regroup. This pause can provide an opportunity for individuals to process their emotions and thoughts, leading to a more productive conversation when it is resumed. Setting a mutually agreed-upon time to revisit the topic can demonstrate a commitment to resolving the issue while respecting the need for space and reflection.

In professional settings, navigating difficult topics often involves addressing issues such as performance feedback, workplace conflicts, or diversity and inclusion. In these contexts, it is important to approach the conversation with professionalism and respect for all parties involved. Providing specific examples and focusing on behaviors rather than personal attributes can help maintain objectivity and prevent defensiveness. Additionally, offering solutions or actionable steps can demonstrate a commitment to positive change and collaboration.

In educational environments, discussing sensitive topics such as race, gender, or mental health requires a thoughtful and inclusive approach. Educators can create a safe and supportive space for these discussions by establishing ground rules for respectful dialogue and encouraging diverse perspectives. Providing context and background information can help students understand the complexity of the issues and foster critical thinking. Additionally, being open to feedback and willing to adapt teaching methods can enhance the learning experience and promote a culture of inclusivity and respect.

## Creating a Safe Space for Vulnerability

Creating a safe space for vulnerability is an essential aspect of fostering genuine connections and promoting personal growth. In a world where individuals often feel pressured to present a façade of strength and invulnerability, providing an environment where people can express their true selves without fear of judgment or ridicule is invaluable. This chapter delves into the principles and practices that can help cultivate such a space, whether in personal relationships, professional settings, or community groups.

At the heart of creating a safe space for vulnerability is the establishment of trust. Trust is the foundation upon which open and honest communication is built. It requires consistency, reliability, and authenticity. When individuals trust that their thoughts and feelings will be respected and valued, they are more likely to share their vulnerabilities. Building trust involves demonstrating integrity, keeping promises, and being transparent in one's intentions. It also means being willing to listen without interrupting or imposing one's own agenda.

Active listening is a crucial component of fostering a safe space. It involves giving full attention to the speaker, acknowledging their emotions, and responding with empathy. Active listening goes beyond merely hearing words; it requires understanding the underlying emotions and intentions. By reflecting back what the speaker has said and asking clarifying questions, listeners can show that they are genuinely engaged and interested in the speaker's perspective. This validation encourages individuals to open up and share more deeply.

Empathy is another key element in creating a safe space for vulnerability. It involves recognizing and validating the emotions of others, even if one does not share the same experiences. Empathy allows individuals to feel seen and understood, reducing feelings of isolation and fear. Expressing empathy can be as simple as acknowledging someone's feelings with phrases like "That sounds really challenging" or

"I can see why you would feel that way." By demonstrating empathy, individuals can create an environment where others feel comfortable expressing their true selves.

Non-judgmental attitudes are essential for fostering vulnerability. When individuals fear being judged or criticized, they are less likely to share their authentic selves. Creating a non-judgmental space involves suspending personal biases and refraining from making assumptions about others' experiences or motivations. It requires an openness to diverse perspectives and a willingness to accept people as they are. By embracing a non-judgmental mindset, individuals can create an inclusive environment where everyone feels valued and respected.

Setting clear boundaries is also important in creating a safe space for vulnerability. Boundaries help define the limits of acceptable behavior and ensure that all parties feel comfortable and respected. Establishing boundaries involves open communication and mutual agreement on what is acceptable and what is not. It also means being willing to enforce those boundaries when necessary. By setting and respecting boundaries, individuals can create a space where everyone feels safe to express themselves without fear of overstepping or being taken advantage of.

In professional settings, creating a safe space for vulnerability can lead to increased collaboration, innovation, and employee satisfaction. Leaders can foster such an environment by modeling vulnerability themselves, sharing their own challenges and uncertainties. This openness can encourage team members to do the same, leading to more authentic and productive interactions. Additionally, providing opportunities for team members to share their thoughts and ideas without fear of retribution can promote a culture of trust and inclusivity.

In educational environments, creating a safe space for vulnerability can enhance learning and personal development. Educators can encourage students to express their thoughts and feelings by creating an atmosphere of respect and acceptance. This can be achieved by establishing ground rules for respectful dialogue, encouraging diverse perspectives, and providing constructive feedback. By fostering a supportive and inclusive environment, educators can help students develop the confidence to explore new ideas and take risks in their learning.

In personal relationships, creating a safe space for vulnerability can deepen connections and strengthen bonds. It involves being present and attentive, offering support and understanding, and being willing to share one's own vulnerabilities. By being open and honest with each other, individuals can build a foundation of trust and intimacy that allows for deeper emotional connections. This mutual vulnerability can lead to more meaningful and fulfilling relationships.

Creating a safe space for vulnerability is not a one-time effort but an ongoing process. It requires continuous reflection, adaptation, and commitment to maintaining an environment of trust and respect. It also involves being willing to address and resolve conflicts or misunderstandings that may arise. By being proactive and intentional in fostering a safe space, individuals can create an environment where vulnerability is not only accepted but celebrated.

# Chapter 4

# Facilitating Personal Growth

## Identifying and Addressing Core Issues

Understanding the root of a problem is often the first step toward finding a meaningful solution. Identifying and addressing core issues requires a keen sense of observation, a willingness to dig deep, and the courage to confront uncomfortable truths. This chapter delves into the process of uncovering these underlying issues, offering practical guidance for those seeking to resolve conflicts, improve relationships, or enhance personal growth.

The journey to identifying core issues begins with self-reflection. Taking the time to examine one's thoughts, feelings, and behaviors can reveal patterns that may point to deeper concerns. This introspection involves asking probing questions about one's motivations, fears, and desires. It requires honesty and a willingness to confront aspects of oneself that may be difficult to acknowledge. By engaging in self-reflection, individuals can gain insight into the underlying factors that influence their actions and decisions.

Once self-reflection has shed light on potential core issues, the next step is to gather information from external sources. This may involve seeking feedback from trusted friends, family members, or colleagues who can provide an outside perspective. These individuals may notice patterns or behaviors that the person themselves may overlook. By listening to their observations and considering their insights, individuals can gain a more comprehensive understanding of the issues at hand.

In some cases, identifying core issues may require professional assistance. Therapists, counselors, and coaches are trained to help individuals explore their thoughts and emotions in a safe and supportive environment. They can provide guidance and tools for uncovering underlying issues and offer strategies for addressing them. Seeking professional help is not a sign of weakness but rather a proactive step toward personal growth and healing.

Once core issues have been identified, the process of addressing them begins. This often involves setting specific, achievable goals that target the underlying concerns. For example, if a core issue is a lack of self-confidence, a goal might be to engage in activities that build self-esteem, such as taking on new challenges or practicing self-compassion. By setting clear goals, individuals can create a roadmap for addressing their core issues and track their progress over time.

Addressing core issues also requires a commitment to change. This may involve altering thought patterns, behaviors, or relationships that contribute to the problem. Change can be challenging, as it often involves stepping outside of one's comfort zone and confronting fears or insecurities. However, by embracing change and remaining open to new possibilities, individuals can create a more fulfilling and authentic life.

In some cases, addressing core issues may involve resolving past traumas or conflicts. This can be a difficult and emotional process, but it is often necessary for healing and growth. Techniques such as journaling, meditation, or therapy can help individuals process and release past experiences that may be holding them back. By letting go of the past, individuals can free themselves to move forward and create a brighter future.

Communication is a vital tool in addressing core issues, particularly in relationships. Open and honest dialogue can help individuals express their needs, desires, and concerns, fostering understanding and connection. Effective communication involves active listening, empathy, and a willingness to compromise. By engaging in meaningful conversations, individuals can work together to address core issues and strengthen their relationships.

In addition to communication, setting healthy boundaries is essential for addressing core issues. Boundaries help define the limits of acceptable behavior and protect individuals from being taken advantage of or overwhelmed. Establishing boundaries involves clearly communicating one's needs and expectations and being willing to enforce them when necessary. By setting and respecting boundaries, individuals can create a safe and supportive environment for addressing core issues.

Addressing core issues is not a one-time event but an ongoing process. It requires continuous reflection, adaptation, and commitment to personal growth. It also involves being willing to revisit and reassess core issues as new challenges and opportunities arise. By

remaining open and flexible, individuals can continue
to evolve and thrive.

## Encouraging Self-Reflection and Insight

Self-reflection is a powerful tool for personal growth
and development, offering individuals the opportunity
to gain insight into their thoughts, emotions, and
behaviors. Encouraging self-reflection involves
creating an environment where individuals feel safe
and supported in exploring their inner world. This
chapter delves into the methods and benefits of
fostering self-reflection and insight, providing
practical guidance for those seeking to deepen their
understanding of themselves and their experiences.

The journey toward self-reflection begins with
creating a space for introspection. This can be a
physical space, such as a quiet room or a peaceful
outdoor setting, or a mental space, where distractions
are minimized, and focus is directed inward.
Establishing a regular practice of setting aside time
for reflection can help individuals develop the habit of
introspection, allowing them to explore their thoughts
and feelings more deeply.

Journaling is a valuable tool for self-reflection,
offering a tangible way to capture and explore one's
inner experiences. By writing down thoughts,
emotions, and observations, individuals can gain
clarity and perspective on their lives. Journaling can
take many forms, from free writing to structured
prompts, and can be tailored to suit individual

preferences and needs. The act of putting pen to paper can help individuals process their experiences and uncover insights that may not be immediately apparent.

Meditation is another effective method for encouraging self-reflection and insight. By quieting the mind and focusing on the present moment, individuals can become more attuned to their inner experiences. Meditation can help individuals develop greater awareness of their thoughts and emotions, allowing them to observe patterns and tendencies without judgment. This heightened awareness can lead to valuable insights and a deeper understanding of oneself.

Engaging in reflective conversations with trusted friends or mentors can also foster self-reflection and insight. These conversations provide an opportunity to explore thoughts and feelings in a supportive and non-judgmental environment. By sharing experiences and receiving feedback, individuals can gain new perspectives and insights that may not be accessible through solitary reflection. These dialogues can also help individuals identify blind spots and challenge assumptions, leading to greater self-awareness.

Artistic expression, such as drawing, painting, or music, can serve as a powerful medium for self-reflection. Creative activities allow individuals to express their inner experiences in a non-verbal way, tapping into emotions and insights that may be difficult to articulate. Engaging in artistic expression can help individuals explore their inner world and gain a deeper understanding of themselves and their experiences.

Self-reflection is not only about exploring one's inner world but also about taking action based on the insights gained. Setting goals and creating action plans can help individuals translate their reflections into meaningful change. By identifying specific areas for growth and development, individuals can create a roadmap for personal transformation. This process involves setting clear, achievable goals and taking deliberate steps toward achieving them.

Developing self-compassion is an essential aspect of self-reflection and insight. It involves treating oneself with kindness and understanding, particularly when facing challenges or setbacks. Self-compassion allows individuals to acknowledge their imperfections and embrace their humanity, fostering a sense of acceptance and self-worth. By cultivating self-compassion, individuals can create a supportive inner environment that encourages growth and insight.

Mindfulness practices can enhance self-reflection by helping individuals stay present and engaged in the moment. Mindfulness involves paying attention to one's thoughts, emotions, and sensations without judgment, allowing individuals to observe their experiences with curiosity and openness. By practicing mindfulness, individuals can develop greater awareness of their inner world and gain valuable insights into their thoughts and behaviors.

# Setting Goals for Personal Development

Setting goals for personal development is a transformative process that empowers individuals to take charge of their growth and progress. It involves identifying areas for improvement, defining clear objectives, and creating actionable plans to achieve them. This chapter delves into the art of goal-setting, offering practical guidance and strategies for those seeking to enhance their personal development journey.

The first step in setting goals for personal development is self-assessment. This involves taking a close look at one's strengths, weaknesses, values, and aspirations. By understanding where you currently stand and where you want to go, you can set meaningful and relevant goals. Self-assessment can be facilitated through various methods, such as introspection, feedback from others, or personality assessments. The key is to gain a comprehensive understanding of yourself and your desires.

Once you have a clear understanding of your starting point, the next step is to define your goals. Effective goals are specific, measurable, achievable, relevant, and time-bound (SMART). Specific goals provide clarity and focus, while measurable goals allow you to track your progress. Achievable goals ensure that your objectives are realistic and attainable, while relevant goals align with your values and long-term aspirations. Time-bound goals create a sense of urgency and help you stay on track.

Breaking down larger goals into smaller, manageable tasks can make the process less overwhelming and more achievable. This approach allows you to focus on one step at a time, building momentum and confidence as you progress. By setting milestones and celebrating small victories along the way, you can maintain motivation and stay committed to your personal development journey.

Creating a detailed action plan is essential for turning your goals into reality. This involves outlining the specific steps you need to take, identifying potential obstacles, and determining the resources and support you may need. An action plan serves as a roadmap, guiding you toward your objectives and helping you stay organized and focused. Regularly reviewing and adjusting your plan can ensure that you remain on track and adapt to any changes or challenges that may arise.

Accountability plays a crucial role in achieving personal development goals. Sharing your goals with a trusted friend, mentor, or coach can provide valuable support and encouragement. These individuals can offer feedback, hold you accountable, and help you stay motivated. Additionally, tracking your progress and reflecting on your achievements can reinforce your commitment and provide a sense of accomplishment.

Embracing a growth mindset is vital for personal development. This mindset involves viewing challenges as opportunities for learning and growth, rather than obstacles to be avoided. By cultivating a growth mindset, you can develop resilience, adaptability, and a willingness to embrace change.

This perspective can help you overcome setbacks and stay focused on your goals, even in the face of adversity.

It's important to recognize that personal development is a lifelong journey, and goals may evolve over time. As you grow and change, your priorities and aspirations may shift, requiring you to reassess and adjust your goals. Regularly revisiting your goals and reflecting on your progress can help you stay aligned with your values and ensure that your objectives remain relevant and meaningful.

Incorporating self-care into your personal development journey is essential for maintaining balance and well-being. Setting goals can be demanding, and it's important to prioritize your physical, emotional, and mental health. By practicing self-care, you can recharge and sustain the energy and motivation needed to pursue your goals. This may involve activities such as exercise, meditation, or spending time with loved ones.

Celebrating your achievements, no matter how small, can boost your confidence and reinforce your commitment to personal development. Acknowledging your progress and accomplishments can provide a sense of fulfillment and motivation to continue striving for your goals. By recognizing and celebrating your successes, you can cultivate a positive and empowering mindset that supports your growth and development.

# Supporting Clients Through Change

Supporting clients through change is a nuanced and multifaceted endeavor that requires empathy, understanding, and strategic guidance. Change, whether anticipated or unexpected, can be a daunting experience for individuals, often accompanied by a mix of emotions ranging from excitement to anxiety. As a professional tasked with guiding clients through these transitions, it is essential to adopt a holistic approach that addresses both the emotional and practical aspects of change.

The journey begins with establishing a strong rapport with the client. Building trust is paramount, as it lays the foundation for open communication and collaboration. This involves actively listening to the client's concerns, validating their feelings, and demonstrating genuine empathy. By creating a safe and supportive environment, clients are more likely to feel comfortable sharing their thoughts and emotions, which is crucial for effective change management.

Understanding the client's unique context is another critical component. Each individual's experience of change is shaped by their personal history, values, and circumstances. Taking the time to explore these factors can provide valuable insights into the client's perspective and inform the development of tailored strategies. This personalized approach ensures that the support provided is relevant and meaningful, increasing the likelihood of a successful transition.

Once a comprehensive understanding of the client's situation has been established, the next step is to collaboratively define clear and achievable goals. These goals should be specific, measurable, and aligned with the client's values and aspirations. By involving the client in the goal-setting process, they are more likely to feel a sense of ownership and commitment to the change. This collaborative approach also empowers clients, fostering a sense of agency and control over their journey.

With goals in place, it is essential to develop a structured action plan that outlines the steps needed to achieve them. This plan should be flexible and adaptable, allowing for adjustments as circumstances evolve. Breaking down larger goals into smaller, manageable tasks can make the process less overwhelming and more attainable. Regularly reviewing and updating the action plan can help maintain momentum and ensure that the client remains on track.

Throughout the change process, it is important to provide ongoing support and encouragement. This can take many forms, from regular check-ins and progress reviews to offering resources and tools that facilitate the transition. Encouraging clients to reflect on their progress and celebrate their achievements can boost confidence and motivation, reinforcing their commitment to the change.

Addressing potential obstacles and challenges is a crucial aspect of supporting clients through change. Anticipating and preparing for these hurdles can help mitigate their impact and prevent setbacks. This may involve identifying potential risks, developing contingency plans, and equipping clients with problem-solving skills. By fostering resilience and adaptability, clients are better equipped to navigate the complexities of change.

Emotional support is equally important in the change process. Change can evoke a range of emotions, from excitement and anticipation to fear and uncertainty. Acknowledging and validating these emotions is essential for helping clients process their feelings and move forward. Encouraging clients to express their emotions and providing a non-judgmental space for them to do so can facilitate emotional healing and growth.

In some cases, clients may benefit from additional support, such as counseling or therapy. Recognizing when to refer clients to other professionals is an important aspect of ethical practice. Collaborating with other experts can provide clients with a comprehensive support network, addressing their needs from multiple angles and enhancing the overall effectiveness of the change process.

As clients progress through their journey, it is important to foster a growth mindset. This involves encouraging clients to view challenges as opportunities for learning and development, rather than insurmountable obstacles. By cultivating a growth mindset, clients can develop resilience and a positive outlook, which can enhance their ability to adapt to change and thrive in new circumstances.

Finally, it is essential to recognize that change is an ongoing process, and clients may require continued support even after their initial goals have been achieved. Encouraging clients to reflect on their experiences and identify areas for further growth can help them maintain momentum and continue their personal development journey. By fostering a culture of continuous improvement, clients can build on their successes and embrace future changes with confidence and optimism.

## Celebrating Progress and Milestones

Recognizing and celebrating progress and milestones is an essential aspect of any journey, whether personal or professional. It serves as a powerful motivator, reinforcing positive behaviors and encouraging continued effort. Celebrations provide an opportunity to reflect on achievements, acknowledge hard work, and foster a sense of accomplishment. This chapter delves into the significance of celebrating progress and milestones, offering practical advice on how to effectively incorporate these celebrations into one's journey.

The journey toward any goal is often fraught with challenges and setbacks. It is easy to become disheartened when faced with obstacles, and the temptation to abandon one's efforts can be strong. Celebrating progress, no matter how small, can serve as a beacon of hope, reminding individuals of how far they have come and reigniting their motivation to persevere. By focusing on progress rather than perfection, individuals can maintain a positive outlook and continue to move forward.

One of the key benefits of celebrating progress is the boost in self-confidence it provides. Acknowledging achievements, even minor ones, reinforces the belief in one's abilities and potential. This increased self-confidence can have a ripple effect, influencing other areas of life and encouraging individuals to take on new challenges with a sense of optimism and determination. By celebrating progress, individuals can cultivate a growth mindset, viewing challenges as opportunities for learning and development.

Milestones, on the other hand, represent significant achievements along the journey. They serve as markers of progress, providing tangible evidence of one's efforts and accomplishments. Celebrating milestones is an opportunity to pause and reflect on the journey thus far, recognizing the dedication and perseverance that have contributed to reaching this point. It is a moment to express gratitude for the support and encouragement received from others, acknowledging the collective effort that has led to success.

Incorporating celebrations into one's journey requires intentionality and creativity. It is important to tailor celebrations to the individual's preferences and values, ensuring that they are meaningful and enjoyable. This may involve organizing a small gathering with friends and family, treating oneself to a special experience, or simply taking a moment to reflect and express gratitude. The key is to create a celebration that resonates with the individual and reinforces the significance of the achievement.

For those who thrive on structure and routine, incorporating regular check-ins and progress reviews can be an effective way to celebrate progress. These check-ins provide an opportunity to assess achievements, set new goals, and identify areas for improvement. By making celebration an integral part of the journey, individuals can maintain a sense of momentum and motivation, continually striving for growth and development.

In a professional context, celebrating progress and milestones can have a profound impact on team dynamics and morale. Recognizing the achievements of team members fosters a culture of appreciation and collaboration, strengthening relationships and enhancing overall productivity. Celebrations can take many forms, from formal recognition ceremonies to informal team gatherings, and should be tailored to the preferences and values of the team.

Leaders play a crucial role in facilitating celebrations within a team or organization. By modeling a culture of appreciation and recognition, leaders can inspire others to adopt similar practices, creating a positive and supportive work environment. This involves actively seeking out opportunities to acknowledge the contributions of team members, providing constructive feedback, and celebrating successes both big and small.

In addition to boosting morale and motivation, celebrating progress and milestones can also serve as a valuable learning opportunity. Reflecting on achievements provides an opportunity to identify the strategies and behaviors that contributed to success, allowing individuals and teams to replicate these practices in the future. It also provides an opportunity to identify areas for improvement, fostering a culture of continuous learning and development.

While celebrating progress and milestones is important, it is equally important to remain grounded and focused on the journey ahead. Celebrations should not be seen as an endpoint, but rather as a stepping stone toward future growth and achievement. By maintaining a balance between celebration and continued effort, individuals can sustain their motivation and momentum, continually striving for excellence.

Incorporating celebrations into one's journey requires a shift in mindset, moving away from a focus on perfection and toward an appreciation of progress. This involves recognizing that growth and development are ongoing processes, and that each step forward, no matter how small, is worthy of celebration. By embracing this mindset, individuals can cultivate a sense of fulfillment and satisfaction, finding joy in the journey itself.

# Chapter 5

# Strategies for Lasting Change

## Developing Resilience and Coping Skills

Resilience and coping skills are essential components of navigating life's challenges and uncertainties. They enable individuals to adapt to adversity, recover from setbacks, and maintain a sense of well-being. Developing these skills is a dynamic process that involves cultivating a mindset of growth and adaptability, as well as acquiring practical strategies for managing stress and adversity. This chapter delves into the importance of resilience and coping skills, offering practical guidance on how to cultivate these attributes in everyday life.

Resilience is often described as the ability to bounce back from adversity. It is not an innate trait, but rather a set of skills and attitudes that can be developed over time. At its core, resilience involves a mindset that embraces change and views challenges as opportunities for growth. This mindset is characterized by optimism, flexibility, and a willingness to learn from experiences. By cultivating a resilient mindset, individuals can approach life's challenges with a sense of confidence and determination.

One of the key components of resilience is the ability to regulate emotions. This involves recognizing and managing one's emotional responses to stress and adversity, allowing for a more balanced and thoughtful approach to problem-solving. Techniques such as mindfulness and meditation can be effective tools for enhancing emotional regulation, providing individuals with the skills to remain calm and focused in the face of challenges.

Social support is another critical factor in developing resilience. Strong relationships with family, friends, and colleagues provide a network of support that can offer encouragement, guidance, and assistance during difficult times. Building and maintaining these connections requires effort and intentionality, but the benefits are substantial. By fostering a sense of community and belonging, individuals can draw strength from their relationships and feel more equipped to handle adversity.

Coping skills are the practical strategies and techniques that individuals use to manage stress and adversity. These skills can be categorized into two main types: problem-focused coping and emotion-focused coping. Problem-focused coping involves taking action to address the source of stress, such as developing a plan to solve a problem or seeking information to better understand a situation. Emotion-focused coping, on the other hand, involves managing one's emotional response to stress, such as practicing relaxation techniques or seeking social support.

Developing effective coping skills requires self-awareness and reflection. It is important for individuals to recognize their own stress triggers and responses, as well as the coping strategies that work best for them. This self-awareness allows individuals to tailor their coping strategies to their unique needs and circumstances, enhancing their ability to manage stress effectively.

One practical approach to developing coping skills is to create a personalized coping toolkit. This toolkit can include a variety of strategies and resources that individuals can draw upon when faced with stress or adversity. For example, the toolkit might include relaxation techniques such as deep breathing or progressive muscle relaxation, as well as activities that promote well-being, such as exercise or creative expression. By having a range of coping strategies at their disposal, individuals can choose the most appropriate approach for each situation.

Resilience and coping skills are not only important for managing stress and adversity, but they also contribute to overall well-being and life satisfaction. By developing these skills, individuals can enhance their ability to navigate life's challenges with grace and confidence, leading to a greater sense of fulfillment and purpose. Moreover, resilience and coping skills can have a positive impact on physical health, as they are associated with lower levels of stress and improved immune function.

In addition to individual efforts, organizations and communities can play a role in fostering resilience and coping skills. Creating environments that promote well-being and support individuals in their efforts to develop these skills can have a profound impact on overall resilience. This might involve offering resources and programs that promote mental health and well-being, as well as fostering a culture of support and collaboration.

# Fostering a Growth Mindset

A growth mindset is a powerful tool that can transform the way individuals approach challenges, learning, and personal development. It is the belief that abilities and intelligence can be developed through dedication, effort, and perseverance. This mindset contrasts with a fixed mindset, where individuals believe that their abilities are static and unchangeable. Embracing a growth mindset can lead to greater motivation, resilience, and success in various aspects of life.

The concept of a growth mindset was popularized by psychologist Carol Dweck, who conducted extensive research on the impact of mindset on achievement and success. Her findings revealed that individuals with a growth mindset are more likely to embrace challenges, persist in the face of setbacks, and view effort as a path to mastery. In contrast, those with a fixed mindset may avoid challenges, give up easily, and see effort as fruitless.

Cultivating a growth mindset begins with self-awareness and reflection. It involves recognizing one's own beliefs and attitudes towards learning and ability. Individuals can start by examining their reactions to challenges and setbacks. Do they view these experiences as opportunities for growth, or do they see them as threats to their self-worth? By becoming aware of these thought patterns, individuals can begin to shift their mindset towards growth.

One practical strategy for fostering a growth mindset is to reframe challenges and setbacks as opportunities for learning and development. This involves changing the narrative around failure and mistakes. Instead of viewing them as indicators of inadequacy, individuals can see them as valuable feedback that provides insights into areas for improvement. This shift in perspective can reduce fear of failure and encourage a more open and curious approach to learning.

Another important aspect of developing a growth mindset is embracing the power of "yet." This simple word can have a profound impact on how individuals perceive their abilities. When faced with a challenge or setback, instead of saying "I can't do this," individuals can say "I can't do this yet." This subtle change in language reinforces the belief that abilities can be developed over time and that success is a matter of effort and perseverance.

Effort is a key component of a growth mindset. Individuals with a growth mindset understand that effort is essential for learning and improvement. They are willing to put in the time and energy required to develop their skills and abilities. This commitment to effort is often accompanied by a sense of curiosity and a desire to explore new possibilities. By embracing effort as a path to mastery, individuals can unlock their potential and achieve greater success.

Feedback is another valuable tool for fostering a growth mindset. Constructive feedback provides individuals with insights into their strengths and areas for improvement. It offers guidance on how to enhance performance and achieve goals. However, receiving feedback can be challenging, especially if it is perceived as criticism. To cultivate a growth mindset, individuals must learn to view feedback as an opportunity for growth rather than a judgment of their worth. By approaching feedback with an open mind and a willingness to learn, individuals can use it to fuel their development.

The environment also plays a significant role in shaping mindset. Supportive environments that encourage exploration, experimentation, and learning can foster a growth mindset. This might involve creating spaces where individuals feel safe to take risks and make mistakes without fear of judgment. It also involves surrounding oneself with people who model a growth mindset and who provide encouragement and support.

Parents, educators, and leaders can play a crucial role in fostering a growth mindset in others. By praising effort, perseverance, and progress rather than innate ability, they can reinforce the belief that abilities can be developed. Encouraging a love of learning and a willingness to embrace challenges can inspire others to adopt a growth mindset.

## Implementing Behavioral Change Techniques

Implementing behavioral change techniques is a transformative process that requires a strategic approach, patience, and persistence. It involves altering habits, attitudes, and behaviors to achieve desired outcomes, whether in personal development, health, or professional settings. Understanding the principles of behavioral change and applying effective techniques can lead to lasting improvements and a more fulfilling life.

The journey of behavioral change begins with self-awareness. Recognizing the need for change and identifying specific behaviors that require modification is the first step. This involves introspection and reflection on one's habits, routines, and patterns. By understanding the underlying motivations and triggers for certain behaviors, individuals can gain insight into the factors that drive their actions. This awareness serves as a foundation for setting clear and achievable goals.

Goal setting is a crucial component of behavioral change. Goals provide direction and purpose, guiding individuals toward their desired outcomes. Effective goals are specific, measurable, achievable, relevant, and time-bound (SMART). By setting SMART goals, individuals can create a roadmap for change, breaking down larger objectives into manageable steps. This approach not only clarifies the path forward but also enhances motivation and commitment.

Once goals are established, it is essential to develop a plan of action. This plan should outline the specific steps and strategies needed to achieve the desired change. It may involve identifying potential obstacles and devising solutions to overcome them. For example, if the goal is to adopt a healthier lifestyle, the plan might include scheduling regular exercise, preparing nutritious meals, and seeking support from friends or family. By having a clear plan, individuals can navigate the challenges of change with confidence and determination.

Behavioral change often requires the development of new habits and routines. Habits are automatic behaviors that are triggered by specific cues or contexts. To create new habits, it is important to identify the cues that trigger the desired behavior and consistently practice the behavior in response to those cues. Over time, the behavior becomes ingrained and automatic. For instance, if the goal is to read more, setting a specific time each day for reading and associating it with a particular cue, such as after dinner, can help establish the habit.

Positive reinforcement is a powerful technique for encouraging behavioral change. It involves rewarding desired behaviors to increase the likelihood of their recurrence. Rewards can be tangible, such as a treat or a new purchase, or intangible, such as praise or a sense of accomplishment. By associating positive outcomes with desired behaviors, individuals can strengthen their motivation and commitment to change. It is important to choose rewards that are meaningful and aligned with personal values to maximize their effectiveness.

Accountability is another key factor in successful behavioral change. Sharing goals and progress with others can provide support, encouragement, and motivation. This might involve enlisting the help of a friend, family member, or coach who can offer guidance and hold individuals accountable for their actions. Regular check-ins and progress updates can help maintain focus and commitment, ensuring that individuals stay on track toward their goals.

Behavioral change is not always a linear process, and setbacks are a natural part of the journey. It is important to approach setbacks with a growth mindset, viewing them as opportunities for learning and growth rather than failures. By analyzing the factors that contributed to the setback and identifying strategies to prevent recurrence, individuals can build resilience and continue moving forward. Flexibility and adaptability are essential, as they allow individuals to adjust their plans and strategies in response to changing circumstances.

Mindfulness and self-compassion are valuable tools for supporting behavioral change. Mindfulness involves being present and aware of one's thoughts, feelings, and actions without judgment. It can help individuals stay focused on their goals and make conscious choices that align with their values. Self-compassion involves treating oneself with kindness and understanding, especially in the face of setbacks or challenges. By cultivating mindfulness and self-compassion, individuals can create a supportive internal environment that fosters change and growth.

Social support and community involvement can also play a significant role in facilitating behavioral change. Engaging with others who share similar goals or interests can provide a sense of belonging and motivation. This might involve joining a group or community that focuses on the desired change, such as a fitness class, book club, or support group. By connecting with others, individuals can share experiences, exchange ideas, and offer mutual support, enhancing their commitment to change.

# Sustaining Motivation and Commitment

Motivation and commitment are the twin engines that drive the journey of personal and professional growth. They are the forces that propel individuals toward their goals, even in the face of obstacles and setbacks. However, sustaining motivation and commitment over the long term can be challenging. It requires a deep understanding of one's intrinsic and extrinsic motivators, as well as the development of strategies to maintain focus and perseverance.

At the heart of sustained motivation lies the concept of intrinsic motivation. This refers to the internal drive to engage in an activity for its own sake, rather than for external rewards or recognition. Intrinsic motivation is fueled by passion, curiosity, and a sense of purpose. To cultivate intrinsic motivation, individuals must connect with their core values and interests. This involves reflecting on what truly matters to them and aligning their goals with these values. When individuals pursue goals that resonate with their authentic selves, they are more likely to experience a sense of fulfillment and joy in the process.

Extrinsic motivation, on the other hand, involves external incentives such as rewards, recognition, or approval from others. While extrinsic motivators can be effective in the short term, they may not sustain motivation over the long haul. To strike a balance between intrinsic and extrinsic motivation, individuals can use external rewards as a complement to their internal drive. For example, setting up a reward system for achieving milestones can provide an additional boost of motivation, while still keeping the focus on the intrinsic value of the goal.

One of the key strategies for sustaining motivation is setting clear and meaningful goals. Goals provide a sense of direction and purpose, helping individuals stay focused on their desired outcomes. To enhance motivation, goals should be specific, measurable, achievable, relevant, and time-bound (SMART). By breaking down larger goals into smaller, manageable steps, individuals can create a sense of progress and accomplishment. This incremental approach not only boosts motivation but also builds confidence and momentum.

Visualization is another powerful technique for maintaining motivation. By vividly imagining the successful achievement of their goals, individuals can create a mental image that inspires and energizes them. Visualization involves engaging all the senses to create a detailed and compelling picture of the desired outcome. This mental rehearsal can enhance motivation by reinforcing the belief in one's ability to succeed and by making the goal feel more tangible and attainable.

Commitment is the steadfast dedication to pursuing one's goals, even when motivation wanes. It involves making a conscious decision to stay the course, regardless of challenges or setbacks. To strengthen commitment, individuals can employ strategies such as accountability and social support. Sharing goals with others and seeking their support can provide encouragement and motivation. This might involve enlisting the help of a mentor, coach, or accountability partner who can offer guidance and hold individuals accountable for their actions.

Creating a supportive environment is also crucial for sustaining motivation and commitment. This involves surrounding oneself with positive influences and minimizing distractions or negative influences that may hinder progress. For example, individuals can curate their physical and digital environments to align with their goals, such as organizing their workspace or limiting time spent on social media. By creating an environment that supports their aspirations, individuals can enhance their focus and determination.

Resilience is an essential quality for maintaining motivation and commitment. It involves the ability to bounce back from setbacks and persevere in the face of adversity. To build resilience, individuals can develop a growth mindset, which is the belief that abilities and intelligence can be developed through effort and learning. By viewing challenges as opportunities for growth and learning, individuals can maintain motivation and commitment even when faced with difficulties.

Self-care is another important aspect of sustaining motivation and commitment. Taking care of one's physical, mental, and emotional well-being is essential for maintaining energy and focus. This might involve prioritizing rest and relaxation, engaging in regular physical activity, and practicing mindfulness or meditation. By nurturing their well-being, individuals can enhance their capacity to stay motivated and committed to their goals.

Celebrating successes and milestones is a valuable strategy for sustaining motivation. Acknowledging and celebrating achievements, no matter how small, can provide a sense of accomplishment and reinforce motivation. This might involve rewarding oneself with a treat or taking time to reflect on the progress made. By recognizing and celebrating successes, individuals can maintain a positive outlook and stay motivated to continue their journey.

## Evaluating and Adjusting Strategies

Strategies are the backbone of any endeavor, whether personal or professional. They provide a roadmap for achieving goals and navigating challenges. However, the dynamic nature of life and work means that strategies must be continually evaluated and adjusted to remain effective. This process of evaluation and adjustment is crucial for ensuring that strategies align with changing circumstances and continue to drive progress.

The first step in evaluating a strategy is to assess its effectiveness. This involves examining whether the strategy is producing the desired outcomes and whether it is being implemented as intended. To do this, individuals can gather data and feedback from various sources, such as performance metrics, stakeholder input, and personal observations. By analyzing this information, individuals can identify areas where the strategy is succeeding and areas where it may be falling short.

One common method for evaluating strategies is the use of key performance indicators (KPIs). KPIs are measurable values that indicate how effectively a strategy is achieving its objectives. By setting specific KPIs at the outset, individuals can track progress and make data-driven decisions about whether to continue, modify, or abandon a strategy. For example, a business might use KPIs such as sales growth, customer satisfaction, or market share to evaluate its marketing strategy.

In addition to quantitative measures, qualitative feedback is also valuable for evaluating strategies. This might involve seeking input from team members, clients, or other stakeholders who are directly impacted by the strategy. By gathering diverse perspectives, individuals can gain insights into the strengths and weaknesses of the strategy and identify potential areas for improvement.

Once a strategy has been evaluated, the next step is to determine whether adjustments are needed. This decision is influenced by several factors, including the degree of alignment between the strategy and the overall goals, the availability of resources, and the external environment. If a strategy is not producing the desired results, it may be necessary to make changes to the approach, tactics, or resources allocated to it.

Adjusting a strategy often involves a process of experimentation and iteration. This means testing new approaches, learning from the outcomes, and refining the strategy based on what works and what doesn't. For example, a company might experiment with different marketing channels to determine which ones are most effective for reaching its target audience. By adopting a mindset of continuous improvement, individuals can adapt their strategies to changing circumstances and maximize their chances of success.

Flexibility is a key attribute when adjusting strategies. The ability to pivot and adapt to new information or unexpected challenges is essential for maintaining momentum and achieving goals. This might involve being open to new ideas, embracing change, and being willing to take calculated risks. By fostering a culture of flexibility and innovation, individuals and organizations can remain agile and responsive in a rapidly changing world.

Communication is another critical component of evaluating and adjusting strategies. Clear and open communication ensures that all stakeholders are informed about the strategy's progress and any changes that may be necessary. This might involve regular updates, meetings, or reports that provide transparency and accountability. By keeping stakeholders engaged and informed, individuals can build trust and support for the strategy and its adjustments.

In some cases, evaluating and adjusting strategies may involve making difficult decisions, such as reallocating resources, changing priorities, or even abandoning a strategy altogether. These decisions require careful consideration and a willingness to let go of approaches that are no longer effective. By focusing on the bigger picture and the ultimate goals, individuals can make strategic decisions that drive long-term success.

The process of evaluating and adjusting strategies is not a one-time event but an ongoing cycle. It requires a commitment to continuous learning and improvement, as well as the ability to adapt to new challenges and opportunities. By regularly assessing the effectiveness of strategies and making necessary adjustments, individuals can ensure that their efforts remain aligned with their goals and continue to deliver value.

# Chapter 6

# The Role of Cultural Sensitivity in Counseling

## Understanding Cultural Influences on Communication

Communication is a complex tapestry woven from the threads of language, gestures, and context. At its core, it is an exchange of information, ideas, and emotions. Yet, the way we communicate is deeply influenced by the cultural frameworks within which we operate. Understanding these cultural influences is essential for effective communication, particularly in an increasingly interconnected world where interactions often span diverse cultural backgrounds.

Culture shapes our perceptions, values, and behaviors, and these, in turn, influence how we communicate. It dictates the norms and conventions that govern interactions, from the words we choose to the nonverbal cues we employ. For instance, in some cultures, direct eye contact is a sign of confidence and honesty, while in others, it may be perceived as disrespectful or confrontational. Similarly, the use of silence can vary significantly across cultures; it might be seen as a sign of thoughtfulness and respect in one context, while in another, it could be interpreted as discomfort or disinterest.

Language is one of the most apparent manifestations of cultural influence on communication. Beyond the literal meanings of words, language carries cultural connotations and nuances that can affect interpretation. Idioms, metaphors, and humor often rely on cultural references that may not translate easily across linguistic boundaries. For example, a phrase that is humorous in one language might be nonsensical or even offensive in another. Understanding these linguistic subtleties requires not only knowledge of the language but also an awareness of the cultural context in which it is used.

Nonverbal communication, including gestures, facial expressions, and body language, is another area where cultural influences are evident. Gestures that are considered friendly or neutral in one culture may have entirely different meanings elsewhere. A thumbs-up gesture, for instance, is generally seen as a positive sign in many Western cultures, but it can be offensive in certain Middle Eastern countries. Similarly, the concept of personal space varies across cultures; what is considered an appropriate distance for conversation in one culture might be perceived as intrusive or distant in another.

Cultural influences also extend to communication styles, which can be broadly categorized as high-context or low-context. High-context cultures, such as those in Japan and many Arab countries, rely heavily on implicit communication and nonverbal cues. In these cultures, much of the meaning is derived from the context of the interaction, including the relationship between the communicators and the setting. In contrast, low-context cultures, such as those in the United States and Germany, prioritize explicit communication, where the message is conveyed primarily through words and is expected to be clear and direct.

Understanding these differences in communication styles is crucial for avoiding misunderstandings and fostering effective cross-cultural interactions. For example, in a high-context culture, a speaker might expect the listener to read between the lines and infer meaning from the context, while a listener from a low-context culture might expect a more straightforward and detailed explanation. Being aware of these differences allows individuals to adapt their communication approach to better align with the cultural expectations of their audience.

Cultural influences on communication are not static; they evolve over time as societies change and interact with one another. Globalization, migration, and technological advancements have all contributed to the blending and reshaping of cultural norms. As a result, individuals may find themselves navigating a complex landscape of cultural influences, where traditional norms coexist with new, hybrid forms of communication.

To effectively navigate this landscape, individuals can develop cultural competence, which involves understanding and respecting cultural differences, as well as adapting communication strategies to suit diverse cultural contexts. This requires an openness to learning about other cultures, as well as a willingness to reflect on one's own cultural biases and assumptions. By cultivating cultural competence, individuals can enhance their ability to communicate effectively across cultural boundaries and build meaningful connections with people from diverse backgrounds.

One practical approach to developing cultural competence is to engage in active listening, which involves paying close attention to both verbal and nonverbal cues and seeking to understand the speaker's perspective. This can help individuals identify cultural nuances and adjust their communication style accordingly. Additionally, asking open-ended questions and seeking clarification can demonstrate respect for cultural differences and facilitate more effective communication.

Another important aspect of cultural competence is empathy, which involves recognizing and appreciating the emotions and experiences of others. By putting oneself in the shoes of someone from a different cultural background, individuals can gain insights into how cultural influences shape communication and develop a more nuanced understanding of the interaction.

In professional settings, cultural competence can be particularly valuable for fostering collaboration and teamwork. Diverse teams bring together individuals with different cultural perspectives, which can lead to innovative solutions and creative problem-solving. However, these benefits can only be realized if team members are able to communicate effectively and navigate cultural differences with sensitivity and respect.

# Adapting Counseling Approaches for Diverse Clients

Counseling is a deeply personal and transformative process, one that requires sensitivity, empathy, and adaptability. As counselors, we are entrusted with the responsibility of guiding individuals through their unique challenges and helping them navigate the complexities of their lives. However, the diversity of clients we encounter means that a one-size-fits-all approach is rarely effective. Each client brings their own cultural background, personal experiences, and individual needs to the counseling session, and it is our duty to adapt our approaches to meet these diverse requirements.

Understanding the cultural context of a client is crucial in tailoring counseling approaches. Culture influences how individuals perceive mental health, express emotions, and seek help. For instance, in some cultures, mental health issues may be stigmatized, leading individuals to avoid seeking professional help. In others, there may be a strong emphasis on community and family support, which can play a significant role in the counseling process. By being aware of these cultural nuances, counselors can create a more supportive and understanding environment for their clients.

Language is another important consideration when adapting counseling approaches. For clients who speak a different language or have limited proficiency in the counselor's language, communication can be a barrier. In such cases, it may be beneficial to work with interpreters or use culturally relevant materials to facilitate understanding. Additionally, counselors should be mindful of the language they use, avoiding jargon or terminology that may be unfamiliar or confusing to the client.

Nonverbal communication is equally significant in the counseling process. Gestures, facial expressions, and body language can convey a wealth of information, but their meanings can vary across cultures. A gesture that is considered positive in one culture may be perceived differently in another. Counselors should be attuned to these nonverbal cues and be willing to adjust their own body language to ensure that they are communicating effectively and respectfully.

Building rapport with clients from diverse backgrounds requires an open and nonjudgmental attitude. Counselors should approach each client with curiosity and a willingness to learn about their unique perspectives and experiences. This involves asking open-ended questions, actively listening, and validating the client's feelings and experiences. By demonstrating genuine interest and respect, counselors can foster a trusting relationship that encourages clients to share openly and honestly.

Flexibility in counseling techniques is essential when working with diverse clients. While some clients may benefit from traditional talk therapy, others may respond better to alternative approaches such as art therapy, music therapy, or mindfulness practices. Counselors should be open to exploring different modalities and be willing to adapt their techniques to suit the client's preferences and needs. This may involve incorporating culturally specific practices or rituals that hold significance for the client.

It is also important for counselors to be aware of their own cultural biases and assumptions. Self-reflection and ongoing cultural competence training can help counselors recognize and address any unconscious biases that may affect their interactions with clients. By acknowledging and challenging these biases, counselors can provide more equitable and effective support to clients from diverse backgrounds.

In addition to cultural considerations, counselors must also be attuned to the individual needs and preferences of each client. This involves taking into account factors such as age, gender, sexual orientation, and socioeconomic status, all of which can influence a client's experiences and perspectives. For example, a young client may have different concerns and communication styles compared to an older client, and a client from a marginalized community may face unique challenges related to discrimination or systemic inequality.

Counselors should also be prepared to address any barriers to accessing mental health services that clients may face. This could include financial constraints, lack of transportation, or limited availability of culturally competent providers. By working collaboratively with clients to identify and address these barriers, counselors can help ensure that clients receive the support they need.

Collaboration with other professionals and community resources can enhance the effectiveness of counseling for diverse clients. Counselors can work with social workers, healthcare providers, and community organizations to provide comprehensive support that addresses the client's holistic needs. This collaborative approach can also help bridge any gaps in services and ensure that clients have access to a network of support.

## Addressing Cultural Misunderstandings

Cultural misunderstandings can arise in various contexts, from casual interactions to professional settings, and they often stem from differences in values, beliefs, and communication styles. These misunderstandings can lead to conflicts, strained relationships, and missed opportunities for collaboration. Addressing cultural misunderstandings requires a nuanced approach that involves awareness, empathy, and effective communication.

One of the first steps in addressing cultural misunderstandings is recognizing that they exist. This may seem straightforward, but cultural differences are often subtle and deeply ingrained, making them easy to overlook. For instance, a gesture or phrase that is considered polite in one culture may be perceived as rude or inappropriate in another. By acknowledging the potential for misunderstandings, individuals can approach cross-cultural interactions with an open mind and a willingness to learn.

Empathy plays a crucial role in bridging cultural gaps. By putting oneself in another person's shoes, it becomes easier to understand their perspective and motivations. This empathetic approach can help diffuse tensions and foster a more collaborative environment. For example, if a colleague from a different cultural background seems unresponsive during meetings, it may be helpful to consider cultural norms around communication and hierarchy. In some cultures, it is customary to defer to authority figures or to avoid speaking out of turn, which may explain the colleague's behavior.

Effective communication is key to resolving cultural misunderstandings. This involves not only verbal communication but also nonverbal cues such as body language, eye contact, and tone of voice. Being mindful of these elements can help prevent misinterpretations and ensure that messages are conveyed accurately. Additionally, active listening is essential in cross-cultural interactions. By paying close attention to what others are saying and asking clarifying questions, individuals can gain a deeper understanding of different perspectives and avoid jumping to conclusions.

Language barriers can also contribute to cultural misunderstandings. When communicating with someone who speaks a different language, it is important to be patient and clear. Avoid using idiomatic expressions or jargon that may be difficult to translate, and be open to using visual aids or gestures to enhance understanding. In some cases, it may be beneficial to work with interpreters or translators to facilitate communication.

Cultural misunderstandings can also arise from differing values and beliefs. For example, in some cultures, individualism is highly valued, while in others, collectivism and community are prioritized. These differences can impact decision-making processes, conflict resolution, and even perceptions of time and punctuality. By being aware of these cultural values, individuals can navigate interactions more effectively and find common ground.

Education and cultural competence training can be valuable tools in addressing cultural misunderstandings. By learning about different cultures and their customs, individuals can develop a greater appreciation for diversity and become more adept at navigating cross-cultural interactions. This knowledge can also help individuals identify and challenge their own biases and assumptions, leading to more inclusive and respectful interactions.

In professional settings, organizations can play a role in fostering cultural understanding by promoting diversity and inclusion initiatives. This may involve creating opportunities for employees to learn about different cultures, encouraging open dialogue about cultural differences, and implementing policies that support diverse perspectives. By creating an inclusive environment, organizations can enhance collaboration and innovation while reducing the likelihood of cultural misunderstandings.

When cultural misunderstandings do occur, it is important to address them promptly and constructively. This may involve having an open and honest conversation with the parties involved, acknowledging any mistakes or misinterpretations, and working together to find a resolution. By approaching these situations with humility and a willingness to learn, individuals can turn misunderstandings into opportunities for growth and connection.

# Promoting Inclusivity and Respect

Inclusivity and respect are foundational elements of a harmonious society, yet achieving them requires intentional effort and commitment. In a world characterized by diversity, promoting these values involves recognizing and valuing the unique contributions of individuals from various backgrounds. It is about creating environments where everyone feels valued, heard, and empowered to contribute their best.

One of the first steps in promoting inclusivity is acknowledging the diversity that exists within any group or community. This diversity can manifest in numerous ways, including race, ethnicity, gender, age, sexual orientation, disability, and socioeconomic status. By recognizing these differences, individuals and organizations can begin to appreciate the richness that diverse perspectives bring to the table. This appreciation is crucial for fostering an inclusive environment where everyone feels welcome.

Creating an inclusive environment also involves actively challenging biases and stereotypes. These preconceived notions can be deeply ingrained and may influence how individuals perceive and interact with others. By becoming aware of these biases, individuals can take steps to counteract them and ensure that their actions and decisions are fair and equitable. This may involve questioning assumptions, seeking out diverse perspectives, and being open to feedback.

Respect is a key component of inclusivity, and it involves treating others with dignity and consideration. This means listening to others' viewpoints, valuing their contributions, and acknowledging their experiences. Respectful interactions are characterized by empathy and understanding, and they create a sense of belonging and acceptance. In professional settings, respect can be demonstrated through inclusive language, equitable opportunities for advancement, and recognition of diverse achievements.

Education and awareness are powerful tools for promoting inclusivity and respect. By learning about different cultures, histories, and experiences, individuals can develop a deeper understanding of the challenges faced by marginalized groups. This knowledge can help individuals become more empathetic and informed allies, advocating for change and supporting initiatives that promote equity and justice.

Organizations play a critical role in fostering inclusivity and respect. By implementing policies and practices that prioritize diversity and inclusion, organizations can create environments where all employees feel valued and supported. This may involve establishing diversity and inclusion committees, providing training on unconscious bias, and setting measurable goals for representation and equity. By holding themselves accountable, organizations can drive meaningful change and set an example for others to follow.

Inclusive leadership is another important aspect of promoting inclusivity and respect. Leaders who prioritize diversity and inclusion create cultures where everyone feels empowered to contribute and succeed. These leaders actively seek out diverse perspectives, encourage open dialogue, and create opportunities for underrepresented groups. By modeling inclusive behavior, leaders can inspire others to do the same and create a ripple effect throughout the organization.

Community engagement is also essential for promoting inclusivity and respect. By building relationships with diverse communities and listening to their needs and concerns, individuals and organizations can work collaboratively to address systemic barriers and create more equitable opportunities. This may involve partnering with community organizations, supporting local initiatives, and advocating for policies that promote social justice.

Promoting inclusivity and respect is an ongoing journey that requires continuous reflection and action. It involves challenging the status quo, embracing change, and being willing to learn from mistakes. By committing to this journey, individuals and organizations can create environments where everyone feels valued and respected, and where diversity is celebrated as a strength.

## Learning from Cultural Perspectives

Understanding and appreciating cultural perspectives can enrich our lives in countless ways. It opens doors to new experiences, broadens our horizons, and fosters empathy and understanding. By learning from cultural perspectives, we gain insights into the diverse ways people interpret the world around them, which can enhance our personal and professional relationships.

One of the most profound ways to learn from cultural perspectives is through storytelling. Stories have been used for centuries to pass down traditions, values, and lessons from one generation to the next. They offer a window into the beliefs and customs of different cultures, allowing us to see the world through the eyes of others. By listening to these stories, we can gain a deeper appreciation for the richness and complexity of human experience.

Travel is another powerful means of learning from cultural perspectives. When we immerse ourselves in a new environment, we are exposed to different ways of living, thinking, and interacting. This firsthand experience can challenge our assumptions and broaden our understanding of the world. Whether it's trying new foods, participating in local customs, or simply observing daily life, travel provides an opportunity to learn and grow.

Language is a key component of culture, and learning a new language can offer valuable insights into the perspectives of its speakers. Language shapes how we think and communicate, and it reflects the values and priorities of a culture. By studying a language, we can gain a deeper understanding of the nuances and subtleties of a culture, as well as the ways in which it differs from our own.

Art and music are also powerful expressions of cultural perspectives. They convey emotions, tell stories, and reflect the values and beliefs of a culture. By engaging with art and music from different cultures, we can gain a greater appreciation for the diversity of human expression. Whether it's a traditional dance, a piece of visual art, or a musical composition, these forms of expression offer a glimpse into the soul of a culture.

Education plays a crucial role in learning from cultural perspectives. By studying history, literature, and social sciences, we can gain a deeper understanding of the forces that have shaped different cultures. This knowledge can help us appreciate the complexities of cultural identity and the ways in which cultures have influenced one another over time. Education also provides the tools to critically analyze and reflect on our own cultural assumptions and biases.

Engaging with diverse communities is another important way to learn from cultural perspectives. By building relationships with people from different backgrounds, we can gain firsthand insights into their experiences and viewpoints. This engagement can take many forms, from participating in cultural events and festivals to volunteering with community organizations. By actively seeking out these opportunities, we can foster meaningful connections and learn from the diversity around us.

In the workplace, learning from cultural perspectives can enhance collaboration and innovation. Diverse teams bring a variety of viewpoints and approaches to problem-solving, which can lead to more creative and effective solutions. By valuing and leveraging these diverse perspectives, organizations can create a more inclusive and dynamic work environment. This requires a commitment to open communication, active listening, and mutual respect.

Learning from cultural perspectives also involves recognizing and challenging our own biases and assumptions. We all have preconceived notions based on our cultural upbringing, and these can influence how we perceive and interact with others. By reflecting on these biases and seeking to understand their origins, we can become more open-minded and empathetic individuals. This self-awareness is essential for building bridges across cultural divides.

Ultimately, learning from cultural perspectives is about embracing diversity and celebrating the richness of human experience. It is about recognizing that there is no single way to view the world, and that each culture offers valuable insights and lessons. By approaching cultural differences with curiosity and respect, we can create a more inclusive and harmonious society.